PELICAN BOOKS

READ BETTER, READ FASTER

MANYA DE LEEUW is a director of Reading Efficiency Training Services. She was formerly on the extra-mural staff of the City University as a lecturer in reading efficiency. She has had wide experience of in-company 'workshops' in reading efficiency with leading commercial and industrial organizations: in areas as varied as accounting, air and road transport, banking, ceramics, chemicals, computing, distributive trades, engineering, insurance, manufacturing, medical research, pharmaceuticals, publishing and shipping. She also conducts intensive workshops in reading efficiency for the Institute of Directors, the Guardian Business Services, universities, professional bodies and local government; and courses for the general public.

ERIC DE LEEUW was formerly Dean of the Faculty of Economics and Administrative Studies at the North-Western Polytechnic, where he led a research team in reading efficiency under the auspices of the Department of Scientific and Industrial Research. He visited the United States as a member of a European Productivity Agency mission to report on management education and training. He is an assessor for the graduate and post-graduate training schemes of the Institution of Industrial Managers. He has given courses in reading efficiency at the House of Commons, the Foreign Office, the Treasury, the Department of Industry and Trade, and other Government ministries; for many years he gave intensive workshops in reading efficiency for the Institute of Directors. He has made contributions to both BBC and ITV.

D0910717

MANYA AND ERIC DE LEEUW

Read Better, Read Faster

A NEW APPROACH TO
EFFICIENT READING

PENGUIN BOOKS

PENGUIN BOOKS

Published by the Penguin Group
27 Wrights Lane, London W8 5TZ, England
Viking Penguin Inc., 40 West 23rd Street, New York, New York 10010, USA
Penguin Books Australia Ltd, Ringwood, Victoria, Australia
Penguin Books Canada Ltd, 2801 John Street, Markham, Ontario, Canada L3R 1B4
Penguin Books (NZ) Ltd, 182–190 Wairau Road, Auckland 10, New Zealand

Penguin Books Ltd, Registered Offices: Harmondsworth, Middlesex, England

First published 1965
21 23 25 27 29 30 28 26 24 22

Made and printed in Great Britain by
Hazell Watson & Viney Limited
Member of BPCC plc
Aylesbury, Bucks, England
Set in Linotype Times

CONTENTS

Part II: The Strategy of Reading

Part III: Additional Exercises

Part IV: How Much Improvement?

Appendices

PREFACE

THIS is a self-training manual for improving efficiency in the reading of *informative* material. It is a manual for readers in general including those in business and the professions, students and sixth-formers; it may also be helpful to teachers of the subject and to anyone interested in written or verbal communication.

Speed has no significance apart from the reader's purpose and interest, his knowledge of the subject, his comprehension, his method of assimilation, his effort, and the nature of the material; the whole emphasis of this book is therefore on purpose, comprehension, and the method of assimilation – in short, *efficiency*. We are concerned with speed because to be efficient is to achieve one's purpose as quickly (and, of course, as easily) as possible.

It has been established beyond a shadow of doubt that readers in general waste a great deal of time and effort. Why is this so? Why is it that the worst readers by any standard are often the ablest of people? Why is it that the majority of students have very little idea how to tackle their reading? Why is it that a high proportion of readers – not excluding those whose professional work entails a lot of reading – use a technique that is no more advanced than when they were children? Or why are there people – to take an extreme but illuminating example – who in conversation and discussion can sustain a difficult argument with ease and yet as readers assimilate only topical information, and even that with difficulty, so that worth-while books are virtually beyond them? In our opinion reading presents technical problems of communication that dispose the reader to use inappropriate methods of assimilation: this, and only this, can provide an adequate explanation of why readers as a class are so inefficient. Our efforts as teachers have been directed to devising simple methods for assisting the

PREFACE

reader to overcome the technical problems of assimilating the printed page, so that his reading may become as active and flexible, yet as natural and relaxed, as intelligent conversation or discussion.

The purpose of this manual is threefold:

1. To provide a complete range of exercises similar to those we use in our courses, with standardized exercises for assessing progress;

2. To explain the psychological processes involved in reading, because we have found that this kind of awareness improves performance by enabling the reader, both consciously and unconsciously, to become his own trainer;

3. To prepare the ground for a psychology of reading – something that is sadly needed.

The accepted evidence is that most people, when tested on short passages, can increase their reading speed by about 50 per cent, usually with better comprehension. But in real situations the tasks of reading, taken as a whole, are complex: the reader has to plan and organize, to select the best method for the particular purpose – in short, to use a strategy of reading. Our aim as teachers has been to widen the scope of the traditional methods of training so as to include the skills involved in the more complex tasks of everyday reading. The improvement in reading speed, according to the ability to comprehend short passages, is truly astonishing; but this increase in efficiency is small in comparison with the saving in time and effort that is possible where the reader has more opportunity to become a strategist; he may, in fact, be able to double or even to treble his volume of reading.

10

INTRODUCTION

OUR approach breaks with traditional methods in two ways. In the first place, we are in complete opposition to the theory that reading can be improved by training the eyes. There is no lack of scientific evidence to show that the eyes cannot be trained to make 'good' movements. Good and bad eye movements are the result of reading habits and are not, themselves, the cause. We shall not consider this topic at the outset; but deal with it fully in Chapter 5. The reason for this delay is that we are convinced that any preoccupation with the eyes, or any attempt to move them more quickly, can do nothing but harm. Secondly, our aim is to develop not only the skills that are required for reading short passages of the kind used in traditional exercises, but also the skills involved in the strategy of reading; and we shall therefore include longer passages that have to be read in different ways, at different speeds, for different purposes.

In real situations the purposes are extremely varied: the reader may need just enough information to establish an order of priority in his reading, or to decide against reading; in some cases he may require a broad outline, in others a full and detailed understanding; he may need specific information or answers to particular questions; he may have to study long articles or books, for which not one but several readings may be the best method; or he may have to read against the clock. All these tasks require different techniques and the reader has to plan his reading according to his purpose. We do not dispute the value of short exercises as a form of basic training; and we find them indispensable for 'measuring' progress; but training must provide more extensive exercises than these, if it is to enable the reader to increase his efficiency in everyday reading.

Our methods are based on principles of learning. Reading is assimilation – LEARNING – and all learning is a digestive process. But the mind can digest so much at a time and no more. If the reader goes twice as fast he assimilates half as much; if he reduces his speed by half he assimilates twice as much. What, then, one might ask, is the point of reading faster? It seems to take as long, in the end, in relation to the amount of information that is assimilated, unless we skimp our reading.

Any approach which emphasizes speed and ignores efficiency has no effective answer to this. But let us consider the position in the light of efficiency. As there is no possibility of increasing the rate at which the brain can clear information, the aim must be to increase the efficiency of reading: to make the fullest possible use of the reader's capacity and to avoid wasting it. The evidence is unmistakable: there is an enormous waste of capacity; some of the most able people are among the least efficient readers. This is largely the result of a technical problem of communication between author and reader by means of the printed word; and from this problem come the main obstacles to efficient reading. This is what happens:

First – the problem of communication. The writer – or, for that matter, the speaker – conceives his thought 'whole', as a unity, but must express it in a line of words; the reader – or listener – must take this line of symbols and from it reconstruct the original wholeness of thought. There is little difficulty in conversation, because the listener receives innumerable cues from the physical expression of the speaker; there is a dialogue, and the listener can cut in at any time. The advantage of group discussion is that people can overcome linear sequences of words by converging on ideas from different directions; which makes for wholeness of thought. But the reader is confronted by line upon line of printed symbols, without benefit of physical tone and emphasis or the possibility of dialogue or discussion. In his very eagerness to master the technical problem, he is prone to memorize, concentrating on the words themselves, looking *at* them instead of looking *for* their meaning; and to the extent that he uses this most inefficient method of learning, his capacity is wasted.

Secondly, assimilation is an active process of relating new information to existing knowledge. If, by memorizing, the reader turns his mind into a passive receptacle for printed words, he cannot use his existing knowledge and his capacity is wasted.

Thirdly, because the rate at which the brain can clear information is limited, the reader must, if he is to read efficiently, *vary* his reading speed, taking more time where the work is heavy and less time where it is light. Reading, therefore, requires a wide range of speed. Readers in general seem to become subdued by the printed word and are not nearly flexible enough in their speed: some appear to have only one speed, whatever their knowledge of the subject or the difficulty of the material. This inflexibility wastes capacity.

Lastly, if the reader becomes passive, he is inclined to mistake or ignore his purpose. Lack of purpose is a great waste of capacity.

Our aim, therefore, is efficient reading. It is perhaps comforting for the reader to know that his eyes need no training: quick results would certainly not be possible if he had to increase his visual capacity. Although the purposes of everyday reading are complex, the requisite skills are not difficult to acquire and the reader can expect quick improvement.

Procedure

The exercises should be spread over a minimum period of six weeks. Skills cannot be improved overnight; and we see no purpose in ploughing through the reading passages one after another. Furthermore, additional practice is necessary if the skills are to be applied proficiently.

The details of the procedures and suggestions for additional practice will be given in the text.

PART I

*

THE PROCESS OF
READING

CHAPTER 1
HOW FAST DO YOU READ?

THE purpose of this chapter is to ascertain your present speed and level of comprehension, and obtain a standard for assessing your progress.

You will read two short passages, find your speed in words per minute, and test your comprehension. (The procedure is given below.) At the end of the book there are two similar exercises, and, by comparing your average speed and average comprehension score for the first two passages with your averages for the last two, you can calculate your increase in speed and comprehension.

You should read the initial exercises in your usual way: if you rush the first passage you may read the second one too slowly; and in any case, for your own satisfaction, you need to know how you are reading now. In the next chapter you will be able to compare your performance with that of other people who have been tested on similar passages.

Procedure
Getting Ready

You need a watch with a second hand, and a pencil or pen. It is usually better to sit at a table, though this depends on what you are used to. See that the light is good and that there is nothing to distract you.

Reading

Your object is to interpret the author's meaning: what he says, not what you feel he should have said.

Timing

Write down the time you start reading. (Allow a few seconds for this.) As soon as you have finished reading, note the time and write it down.

Answering the Questions

Each reading passage in this book is followed by a comprehension test, which you should complete without referring back to the text. The kind of test varies but you will always be told what to expect. The test for each of the passages you are about to read consists of ten questions; four possible answers are given to each question; you have to select the best answer to each question and put a, b, c, or d in the space provided. It may happen that two or more of the possible answers are relevant; if so, you must decide which of them is most relevant. There is one mark for each question, a total of ten.

The answers to these 'multiple-choice' questions, as they are called, are given in the Key in Appendix I.

Your Speed in Words per Minute

After you have answered and checked the questions, calculate your reading time in seconds from the times you have written down. When you have done this you can obtain your speed in words per minute from the Table of Speeds in Appendix III.

Your Comprehension Score

For the purposes of training, 7 is a satisfactory score. This is your working standard. You are not taking an intelligence test; your score is a measure of your comprehension in relation to your speed, your method of reading, and many other factors.

Exercise 1 (910 words)

ENDS AND MEANS

Extract from *Authority and the Individual** by Bertrand Russell

starting time 11:45:00

To strike the right balance between ends and means is both difficult and important. If you are concerned to emphasize means, you may point out that the difference between a civilized man and a savage, between an adult and a child, between a man and an animal, consists largely in a difference as to the weight attached to ends and means in conduct. A civilized man insures his life, a savage does not; an adult brushes his teeth to prevent decay, a child does not except under compulsion; men labour in the fields to provide food for the winter, animals do not. Forethought, which involves doing unpleasant things now for the sake of pleasant things in the future, is one of the most essential marks of mental development. Since forethought is difficult and requires control of impulse, moralists stress its necessity, and lay more stress on the virtue of present sacrifice than on the pleasantness of the subsequent reward. You must do right because it is right, and not because it is the way to get to heaven. You must save because all sensible people do, and not because you may utimately secure an income that will enable you to enjoy life. And so on.

But the man who wishes to emphasize ends rather than means may advance contrary arguments with equal truth. It is pathetic to see an elderly rich business man, who from work and worry in youth has become dyspeptic, so that he can eat only dry toast and drink only water while his careless guests feast; the joys of wealth, which he had anticipated throughout long laborious years, elude him, and his only pleasure is the use of financial power to compel his sons to submit in their turn to a similar futile drudgery. Misers, whose absorption in

* © Bertrand Russell, 1949. Reproduced from *Reith Lectures 1948–1949* by permission of George Allen & Unwin, London, and Simon & Schuster Inc., New York.

means is pathological, are generally recognized to be unwise, but minor forms of the same malady are apt to receive undue commendation. Without some consciousness of ends, life becomes dismal and colourless; ultimately the need for excitement too often finds a worse outlet than it would otherwise have done, in war or cruelty or intrigue or some other destructive activity.

Men who boast of being what is called 'practical' are for the most part exclusively preoccupied with means. But theirs is only one-half of wisdom. When we take account of the other half, which is concerned with ends, the economic process and the whole of human life take on an entirely new aspect. We ask no longer: what have the producers produced, and what has consumption enabled the consumers in their turn to produce? We ask instead: what has there been in the lives of consumers and producers to make them glad to be alive? What have they felt or known or done that could justify their creation? Have they experienced the glory of new knowledge? Have they known love and friendship? Have they rejoiced in sunshine and the spring and the smell of flowers? Have they felt the joy of life that simple communities express in dance and song? Once in Los Angeles I was taken to see the Mexican colony – idle vagabonds, I was told, but to me they seemed to be enjoying more of what makes life a boon and not a curse than fell to the lot of my anxious hard-working hosts. When I tried to explain this feeling, however, I was met with a blank and total lack of comprehension.

People do not always remember that politics, economics, and social organization generally, belong in the realm of means, not ends. Our political and social thinking is prone to what may be called the 'administrator's fallacy', by which I mean the habit of looking upon a society as a systematic whole, of a sort that is thought good if it is pleasant to contemplate as a model of order, a planned organism with parts neatly dovetailed into each other. But a society does not, or at least should not, exist to satisfy an external survey, but to bring a good life to the individuals who compose it. It is in the individuals, not in the whole, that ultimate value is to be sought. A good society is a means to a good life for those who compose it, not something having a separate kind of excellence on its own account.

When it is said that a nation is an organism, an analogy is being used which may be dangerous if its limitations are not recognized. Men and the higher animals are organisms in a strict sense: whatever good or evil befalls a man befalls him as a single person, not this or that part of him. If I have toothache, or a pain in my toe, it is *I* that have the pain, and it would not exist if no nerves connected the part concerned with my brain. But when a farmer in Herefordshire is caught in a blizzard it is not the government in London that feels cold. That is why the individual man is the bearer of good and evil, and not, on the other hand, any collection of men. To believe that there can be good or evil in a collection of human beings, over and above the good or evil in the various individuals, is an error; moreover, it is an error which leads straight to totalitarianism, and is therefore dangerous.

finishing time 11:49:36

QUESTIONS

1 The author maintains that (a) our ends must be worthy; (b) we should concentrate on ends; (c) our means should have value in themselves; (d) to strike a right balance between means and ends is both difficult and important. (*d*)

2 One of the most essential marks of mental development is (a) to eradicate impulse; (b) to exercise forethought; (c) to do right because it is right and not because it is the way to get to heaven; (d) to behave rationally (*b*)

3 Without some consciousness of ends, the need for excitement may lead ultimately to (a) destructive activities; (b) a pathological absorption in means; (c) the selfish pursuit of wealth and power; (d) forms of escapism that are apt to be commended. (✗) *a*

21

4 Men who boast of being what is called 'practical'
(a) usually feel the joy of living; (b) succeed in business because they have a purpose; (c) are for the
most part exclusively preoccupied with means; (d)
become dyspeptic from work and worry.   (C)

5 According to the author, the Mexican colony in Los
Angeles (a) were idle vagabonds; (b) seemed to enjoy life better than his American hosts; (c) were
good Americans; (d) were anxious and hard-working.   (b)

6 The author reminds us that politics, economics, and
social organization generally are concerned with (a)
ends; (b) means; (c) social welfare; (d) people.   (b)

7 The 'administrator's fallacy' is the habit of (a) forgetting that systems change; (b) concentrating on the
specialized parts at the expense of the whole; (c) forgetting that only people can make the most perfect
system work; (d) looking upon society as a systematic whole.   (d)

8 Ultimate value is to be sought in (a) right conduct;
(b) the glory of new knowledge; (c) individuals; (d)
society as a whole.   (C)

9 The good society (a) is a means to a good life for
those who compose it; (b) should have a separate
kind of excellence on its own account; (c) should be
a model of order; (d) is an illusion.   (a)

10 A dangerous error is to believe that (a) fundamen-
tally man is good; (b) a part of man is essentially
evil; (c) there can be good or evil in a collection of
human beings, over and above the good or evil in
the various individuals; (d) the individual rather
than society should decide what is good or evil.   (C)

---

speed.200.w.p.m. (page 240) comprehension....9.... (page 235)

---

time : 4:36

Exercise 2 (900 words)

THE FIGHT AGAINST THE DOWRY*
by Lynne Edmunds – *Guardian*, August 1962

starting time 11:59:00

Few of the British tourists flocking to Greece realize that the strikingly attractive women they admire, whether in city streets or in country villages, have little chance to enjoy their legal independence. It is the traditional demand for a dowry that plays a greater part than the observance of any other custom in keeping Greek women in servility.

The rigid family law that kept daughters at home, sheltered from outside influence until a suitable marriage was arranged, was relaxed for the first time during the Second World War when Greek women took over so many duties. In 1952 they won the vote and in 1957 were given the legal right to enter any profession, excepting the Church and the Army. Already, by 1957, women made up 23 per cent of the students attending universities.

Nevertheless, in a country with a million registered as unemployed or underemployed, even these professional women find themselves completely dependent on family financial support. It is partly because Greek women are unable to make any personal contribution to the setting up of their own homes that the custom of the dowry persists.

When the girl, or more often the family itself, has arranged a suitable match, the prospective husband asks for a settlement. The actual dowry can vary from a herd of goats in a country village to £3,000 or a fully furnished house in the town. Unless special provisions are made, the wife has no legal right to any share of it. If a financial agreement cannot be reached then the marriage is called off.

'Generally the suitors assess the family resources in advance, and ask for as much as they think they can get,' explained Mrs Bella Kilimi, a social worker who has studied the effects of the

* Reproduced by permission of the author.

custom during her seven years with the Ministry of Social Service. Many men choose their wives for the large dowries they bring and not for their personal qualities. Even the unattractive, the crippled, and the simple-minded, can be married off if their families are wealthy enough. On the other hand, daughters of poorer parents often have to take husbands out of their age group or out of their class.

Since a father has the power to withhold or reduce his daughter's dowry, he can easily restrict her freedom of choice in marriage and exert pressure to persuade her into marrying the family's candidate. Many educated women in their middle and late twenties find themselves financially dependent and so forced to accept this situation and to conform to the family ruling that they should not smoke, drink, or meet men friends unchaperoned.

'There is no place in our culture for the casual friendships that result in the choice of a suitable partner,' said Mrs Helene Kalfoglou, programme director at the Thessaloniki YWCA centre. 'Girls from poorer families are anxious to find a "cheap" husband and are likely to marry the first man the family can afford.'

The dowry custom is widespread in urban and rural areas alike, and the YWCA programme is geared to tackling the problem on a nation-wide scale. Its aim is to help girls towards independence by providing them with an educational programme. 'The 7,000 members who attend our main centres in Athens and Thessaloniki, and our rural centres throughout Greece, are taught commercial subjects, languages, hairdressing, hotel work, crafts, and cooking,' explained Mrs Kalfoglou.

Greek girls are anxious to be educated, so anxious, in fact, that in recent years they have outnumbered the men in the philosophy, theology, and dentistry departments of the universities. Now the philosophy department has a fifty-fifty ruling, while in the other faculties, with the exception of law and mathematics, the ratio is kept at one girl for every three boys.

Mrs Maria Thanopoulos, president of the Greek Association for Women's Rights and a practising lawyer in Athens, is determined to continue her thirty-year struggle for female equality until the dowry is replaced by a system of community property and equal pay is accepted.

'These principles go hand in hand,' said Mrs Thanopoulos, 'for as women become financially independent they will be able to contribute towards the setting up of their own homes and the dowry will die. However, progress will be slow, for there is not enough work for our men, and women only get preference in the branches of private industry where they are paid 25 per cent less for the same work. In public service we have won equal pay,' she added, 'but the large number of women in the lower grades thins out to a very small representation in responsible posts. We are still fighting prejudice.'

The Greek system of separate polling stations makes it possible to discover that Greek women are thinking for themselves and generally voting differently from their menfolk, but Mrs Lina Tsaldaris, widow of a former Prime Minister and herself one of the MPs for Athens, emphasized that the strength and influence of the family had not decreased. 'It is very rarely that a girl marries without her parents' consent,' she said. 'But I feel that in the cities the demand for dowries is declining.'

Undoubtedly it will continue to decline as the country's employment situation improves, but in a situation where even professional men have to wait until the age of 30, or even 40, before they can afford to marry, the change will come slowly.

---

finishing time |2 : 03 : 45

QUESTIONS

1 Greek women (a) have no legal rights; (b) are excluded by law from most professions; (c) have little chance to enjoy their legal independence; (d) are not interested in legal independence. (c)

2 The effect of unemployment has been (a) to make even professional women dependent on family financial support; (b) to revive the dowry system; (c) to increase the number of unmarried women; (d) to weaken the dowry system. (ᵈ) a

25

3   The dowry is (a) confined largely to the rural districts; (b) primarily an institution of the middle classes; (c) not required if the woman is sufficiently attractive; (d) a financial agreement on which marriage everywhere depends. (d)

4   We can infer that arranged marriages (a) are customary everywhere in Greece; (b) are rare among professional women; (c) are prevalent only among wealthy families; (d) are fast disappearing. (a)

5   The YWCA is engaged in a nation-wide campaign (a) to fight the prejudice against education for women; (b) to help girls towards independence by means of an educational programme; (c) to provide Christian education; (d) to prepare women for marriage. (b)

6   Greek women at universities (a) account for only three per cent of the number of students; (b) find it easier than others to have casual friendships that lead to marriage; (c) outnumber men in certain departments; (d) are usually there because they cannot get married. (c)

7   Women who work (a) are usually in family businesses; (b) get equal pay; (c) get less pay, except in public service; (d) earn less than men everywhere. (d)c

8   Politically, Greek women (a) show little interest; (b) adopt the views of their husbands; (c) are thinking for themselves; (d) have no rights. (c)

9   The power of the family (a) is declining as women become better educated; (b) is declining fast, particularly in the cities; (c) is more tyrannical than ever; (d) has not decreased. (d)

10 The demand for dowries (a) has greatly diminished, because families cannot afford them; (b) is declining in the cities; (c) is increasing everywhere to offset the fear of unemployment; (d) is declining everywhere, because of the growing freedom between the sexes. (b)

speed...190....w.p.m. (page 240) comprehension...8...... (page 235)

4:45 (285)

Recording Your Progress

Enter your reading speeds and comprehension scores in the Record Sheet on page 245. Your comprehension score should be recorded as a percentage, which is obtained by multiplying the score by ten.

Assessing Your Progress

Do not expect a steady upward trend in your reading speed: progress may be slow at first. For most readers the real improvement seems to come about two-thirds of the way through the course; though it may occur suddenly and quite unexpectedly at any stage. The majority of readers are likely to make most progress when they do the exercises in Part III.

Apart from the initial and final exercises, which have been standardized, the material varies in length, difficulty, and content, and the comprehension tests are of different kinds; for this reason alone, the recorded speeds will fluctuate. One or two passages are for slow reading, because the purpose is to practise a method, and the emphasis is on the saving of time and effort, rather than on an increase in speed; other passages have to be read in such a way that efficiency is reflected in speeds that are well above the average. All this must be taken into account when you assess your progress. Furthermore, as the passages have been made as varied as possible, your results will depend to some extent on the nature of your interests; it is not unusual for a reader to experience great difficulty with an exercise that other readers find easy.

You will see, therefore, that the Record Sheet has to be interpreted. The best guide is your personal assessment of your achievement; you will soon be able to tell whether you are reading better or not. But you should find, given your particular interests, that some passages are of a similar standard; and you should be able to make a number of comparisons. The exercises in Part III should give you the clearest indication of progress.

CHAPTER 2

READING SPEEDS

Slow, Medium, or Fast?

HERE is an estimate of the speeds of the general reading public, for passages comparable to those you have just read.

Scale of Speeds in Words per Minute

170–200	Very slow
200–230	Slow
230–250	Average
250–300	Above average
300–350	Medium-fast
350–450	Fast
450–550	Very fast
550–650	Exceptionally fast

In 1956, in a research project at the North-Western Polytechnic under the auspices of the Department of Scientific and Industrial Research, Miss K. Napier and E. F. Hart tested 147 readers: eighty-two in business groups and sixty-five in classes for the general public. The average initial speed was 232 w.p.m. The speed of the business groups was 223 w.p.m.; and that of the general public, 241 w.p.m. The classification of these readers according to their initial speeds showed that two-thirds were within the range 200–300 w.p.m.

Initial Speeds of 147 Readers

Words per minute	Under 200	200–239	240–269	270–299	300–319	320–359	360–399	Above 400
Number of readers	15	51	28	22	12	12	6	1

Subsequent records have confirmed an average initial speed of 230–250 w.p.m. for the general public, though that of business groups varies a good deal.

For classes of students at Harvard University the average initial speed has been given as 220 w.p.m. This figure is probably too low: it is based on *one* reading passage, and readers, being unfamiliar with the procedure of testing, tend to read the first passage somewhat too slowly.

Our own experience has been mainly with particular occupational groups, which have shown a wide range of average initial speeds, the highest being 380 w.p.m. for a group of nineteen public administrators.

Increasing Our Efficiency

Most readers seem to improve at least two grades on our Scale of Speeds. Readers attending our courses have had an average increase in speed of 60 per cent, with an improvement in comprehension of about 10 per cent.

We have come to regard 250 w.p.m. as a critical speed: below this, we are prepared for slower progress; above this, we reckon on fairly quick improvement. We sometimes find, however, that the reader who is very fast, when he starts the course, is set in his ways, with one speed for everything; he has to learn how to slow down before he can think of speeding up, which is not the easiest adjustment to make. As teachers, we find the *easiest* results are obtained with medium-fast readers: a group of ten psychiatrists started with an average speed of 334 w.p.m. (comprehension 78 per cent) and finished with an average speed of 647 w.p.m. (comprehension 85 per cent).

We decry too much emphasis on absolutes of speed. What matters ultimately is efficiency – the ability to get through the day's work without wasting time and effort; we have known slower readers who could outdistance faster readers when it came to lengthy articles and books, because of their superior skill in planning and organizing. What is often overlooked is that all readers, whether slow or fast, can command an astonishing range of skimming speeds that are quite easy to acquire; and skimming, as we shall see in Chapter 6, is capable of innumerable applications, on which the broad strategy of reading depends.

The aim is to improve the general efficiency of reading. Most readers can double their efficiency – as distinct from their speed – and this is a modest estimate.

General and Specialized Readers

As teachers we have come to distinguish between two broad categories, according to occupation: *general readers*, such as administrators, non-technical managers, publishers, librarians, housewives; and *specialized readers*, such as technologists of all kinds, lawyers, doctors, statisticians, accountants. We have found more fast readers in the general than in the specialized category; and more slow readers in the specialized than in the general category.

The Occupational Hazard

The American psychologist, Robert Woodworth, reports that his colleague, Harold Schlosberg, during an 'open-house' in the laboratory, recorded the eye movements of visitors. In three cases he was 'shocked' by what he saw: evidence of exceptionally slow reading; the three readers were American judges. As we write this, however, we are reminded of a lawyer who read his first test passage at nearly 600 w.p.m., so it is impossible to make predictions about individuals, because private reading interests are more important than vocational activities. Nevertheless, the evidence of our numerous records is unmistakable and needs explaining.

The work of specialists is detailed and analytical; and the reading that is associated with it is necessarily slow. It seems that the slower speeds of specialists are often transferred to reading where faster speeds are more appropriate. Woodworth observes that the judges had carried over their habit of meticulous reading to the laboratory tests, where it was out of place. Slow, inflexible reading is, in our opinion, something of an occupational hazard.

Our conclusion is that there are no absolutes of good or bad reading; there are reading speeds appropriate to particular purposes and different kinds of material. The need is for *flexibility*.

Changing Our Habits

Readers on courses undertake the seemingly impossible task of changing the habits of a lifetime in a few weeks. They are surprised to learn that they can confidently expect to increase their speed by 40 to 60 per cent and double their general efficiency; and even more surprised when they hear that success depends on their own efforts – no 'treatment', no devices for improving vision, no machinery for training the eyes to move in ways that automatically improve performance.

Readers are forthcoming about their reactions to the course. A member explained to his group that having had convincing proof that mechanical aids were so much gimmickry, he had promptly bought one, impelled by a need for treatment. Readers often have to overcome deep-seated resistances, which they discuss freely in retrospect. Reading habits become part of one's ego, one's status as an intelligent self-respecting person; and there is an unconscious inclination to defend this status. Another difficulty, which is real enough, however ridiculous it may sound, is what we might call reader's conscience or the sanctity of the printed word: some readers feel most uncomfortable if they do not read every word, have a sense of guilt about skipping or skimming, and feel duty-bound to finish whatever they have started, however distasteful and unnecessary the task.

Problems are bound to arise with sudden changes in established habits. Some readers change their habits quite successfully, but remain sceptical about the results even when there is convincing evidence of improvement. So it is not infrequent for a member of a course to read much faster than usual and be quite satisfied until he is told his speed, when he will protest that he cannot have understood the passage; he may even write a perfect summary and still believe he has missed a great deal.

We have mentioned these points to give you an insight into

the problems of other readers because, not being a member of a course, you may imagine that for others progress is all plain sailing. Initial difficulties are common; but they are soon overcome with a little perseverance.

A Note on Comprehension Tests

In this book we use three types of comprehension test: multiple-choice questions, free-answer questions, and the summary.

Multiple-choice Questions

These are a convenient method of testing on account of the simple and precise procedure. They are easy in the sense that they are *recognition* tests; for it is easier to recognize than to recall. They are difficult in the sense that they are *arbitrary*, the pattern of comprehension being decided for the reader, who may not agree with the way the text has been questioned; the reader who resents this violence to his judgement may easily drop a point or two.

As they are recognition tests they assess *minimal comprehension*; and the imaginative reader with a score of eight or nine may have understood the essential meaning better than the less imaginative reader with a score of ten. On the other hand they do not favour the mere memorizing of words, because if the possible answers follow the wording of the text very closely, the reader who has not read with understanding may find them bewildering.

On the whole, readers who are good at one kind of test are good at others. In practice multiple-choice questions are a satisfactory measure of the basic comprehension of short passages where the meaning is spread fairly evenly; they are therefore valuable for basic training. They cannot, however, be used for longer passages requiring a high degree of selectivity in reading.

Free-answer Questions

The reader answers a number of set questions in his own words. This is a good test of comprehension because he cannot rely on recognition and the questions cover broader aspects of the text. There is still an element of arbitrariness, though this depends on the number of questions, and how they are framed; properly constructed, however, free-answer questions are a fair and flexible method of testing because the number of questions can be varied to suit any length of passage.

The difficulty is in assessing the answers: comprehension is always a matter of judgement and there can be no infallible standard. This problem is common to all examinations and is something we have to accept. (It is even present in multiple-choice questions, where there may be genuine disagreement about the choice of the most relevant answer.)

The Summary

There is nothing arbitrary about this: the reader decides the amount and the kind of information he requires; he can therefore read freely and flexibly. Furthermore, he must be able to retain and recall the information: if he cannot do so, then his technique of reading is at fault. The summary, as we shall see, brings home the point that reading requires strategy.

The difficulty is in specifying the purpose of the reading (opinions may differ, for example, about what is meant by 'the main points', 'a general understanding', 'a detailed understanding'), and in assessing the summary. Moreover, additional skills are involved in writing a summary and these are, to some extent, being tested as well. Despite these difficulties the summary is the best test of comprehension; and the longer passages in Part II are tested in this way. We strongly recommend that when there are multiple-choice or free-answer questions the reader should note down the main points before answering the questions, or at any rate make a mental summary.

What to Do Next

Reading

The next two passages contain plenty of illustrations and examples. One of the best exercises in quick comprehension is to read material containing illustrations and examples, which, by reinforcing the main points, help the reader to get at the meaning behind the words. Many instances of poor comprehension and needlessly slow reading are caused by over-concentration on the words as such: out of context, words are empty symbols. *The first requirement of good, quick comprehension is to read for the meaning behind the words.*

Comprehension

Remember that *for the purposes of training* 7 is a satisfactory score; this is your working standard. If, however, you have read the last two passages very fast, averaging over 400 w.p.m. with satisfactory comprehension, you should make 8 your standard.

The comprehension tests for the next passages are the same type as before – ten multiple-choice questions. *As you correct your answers, you should examine the text.*

Exercise 3 (970 words)

TEARS

Extract from *The Age of Scandal** by T. H. White

---

starting time 11 : 42 : 00

Humans have a faculty for believing that their own fashions are right and proper, and that these have been ordained to exist as such since the beginning of time. We have a fashion in the twentieth century of considering tears to be unmanly, so we assume that they have always been effeminate. But there have been periods when it has been correct for males to cry, and when males have cried, loud and long, about a surprising variety of subjects to the applause and even to the admiration of their friends.

In Chaucer, both sexes weep indiscriminately: Troilus cried,

* © T. H. White, 1951. Reproduced by permission of Jonathan Cape, London; G. P. Putnam's Sons, New York; and International Authors N.Y.

and so did the tedious paladins, Palamon and Arcite. Almost every bruiser in the *Morte d'Arthur* would burst into tears sooner or later, and Lancelot wept 'as he had been a child that had been beaten'. The first lachrymose period seems to have reached without interruption to the days of Shakespeare, when there was a light swing in the opposite direction. 'Albeit unused to the melting mood', the tragic hero then explained, with a hint of apology, before proceeding to shed his tears as fast as the Arabian tree her medicinable gum. Curiously enough, the reaction against the accepted fashion began on the continent at about the same time, and Sancho Panza was always boasting that he was not a crying man. There followed a brief Elizabethan or Caroline interlude, when only women and schoolboys who had been whipped were expected to blubber.

It was in the Age of Scandal, however, that a strange unlikelihood began to appear. The eighteenth century, that unromantic, tea-drinking, Pope-reading, road-middling, classical age: surely we would not have expected such dry old sticks as lived in that to cry? But they howled. More than the most dramatic Elizabethans, publicly, for little or nothing, the duelling gentlemen sobbed their eyes out whenever they could. They wrote proudly to Gray, telling him that they had cried on every page of his Elegy. They wailed over the sentimental Sterne. They quarrelled with old friends in the House of Commons, and were led out, in floods of tears, by admiring supporters. . . .

The jealousy of accomplished weepers came to a head in Fanny Burney, who became positively cattish about an unfortunate girl called Sophy Streatfield, because the latter was able to cry at will. It was because Fanny herself was probably the second-best weeper in the kingdom, and could not endure to be beaten. (The third-best weeper was Anna Seward who, on revisiting her father's rectory in 1793, 'could not restrain the gushing tears, through almost the whole of the five hours I passed in that dear village'.) Large tracts of Fanny's employment at Court were passed in tears, which she recorded with relish. When a harmless mad woman had attempted to stab the King with a blunt table knife, without doing him any harm whatever, 'the Queen glanced round upon the Duchess of Ancaster and Lady Charlotte Bertie, both of whom had burst into tears. "How I envy you!" she exclaimed; "I cannot cry!"' The news was reported in the Palace, and there was not 'a dry eye in either of the Lodges, on the recital of his danger'. At the evening concert, 'the Princess wept continually. The Queen still more deeply struck, could only from time to time hold out her hand to the King, and say – "I have you yet!" ... When I went to the Queen at night, she scarce once opened her lips. Indeed, I could not look at her without feeling the tears ready to start into my eyes'.

The real howl came when George went mad. That old horror Thurlow, a Lord Chancellor of even more duplicity than most Lords Chancellor, spoke to the House 'in a state of agitation which continued till a flood of tears came to his relief' – he happened to be lying – and, when allowed to visit the lunatic monarch, he came out 'so extremely affected ... that the tears rolled down his cheeks, and his feet had difficulty to support him'. At Windsor the Queen glided down a passage 'drowned in tears' and 'the footmen, the housemaids, the porter, the sentinels, all cried, even bitterly, as they looked on'. It was as bad when the King got better, for his loyal subjects began to celebrate. 'I assure you' wrote Fanny proudly, 'I cried twenty times in the day'.

This was strange when one comes to think of it, and unlike what ought to have been expected in an un-Romantic age. It was only when the Romantics themselves came along, that people began to dry their eyes. Here again, it was the opposite of the expected. It was the Romantics who began to frown on masculine emotion. They still wept a good deal, but uneasily, like Othello. By Tennyson's time, people felt shame-faced when they did so. 'Tears, idle tears', they had to explain uncomfortably, before they could let them flow. Unpoetical people even tried to hide them under the bedclothes.

> Oh, would I were dead now,
> Or up in my bed now,
> To cover my head now
>   And have a good cry!

In the end, it was positively asserted, even by the poets, that weeping in males was not to be the thing. They were to work instead. For men must work, stated Charles Kingsley firmly, and women must weep, and the sooner it's over, the sooner to sleep. The fiat had gone forth, under which we labour today.

But will the fashion continue? There have been more sobbing centuries in the past, than there have been stoical ones. If this little history of emotion is accurate then the changes from one fashion to the other have generally happened under a Queen – under Elizabeth, Anne, or Victoria. Are we ourselves, under some future Elizabeth II, to revert to tears? ... It is to be hoped so.

---

finishing time 11:46:23

QUESTIONS

1 In the twentieth century the attitude of regarding tears as womanly (a) is becoming less fashionable; (b) has led us to believe that tears have always been effeminate; (c) is more pronounced than ever before; (d) is making everyone less demonstrative. (b)

2 From Chaucer to Shakespeare (a) only men of quality wept; (b) both sexes wept indiscriminately; (c) men's tears were largely a literary convention; (d) attitudes to weeping changed frequently. (b)

3 In the days of Shakespeare (a) men still wept but there was a light swing in the opposite direction; (b) only women, children, and poets wept; (c) men's tears were confined to the stage; (d) there was a violent reaction against weeping. (a)

4 In the unromantic eighteenth century men howled (a) as a change from tea-drinking, Pope-reading, and classical road-middling; (b) for little or nothing; (c) over politics, duelling, public executions, and great national events; (d) mainly because of the influence of Gray's 'Elegy'. (b)

5 Fanny Burney was (a) a friendly, charitable weeper;

37

(b) second only to the Queen as a weeper; (c) by far
the most accomplished weeper in the kingdom; (d)
perhaps the second-best weeper in the kingdom, and
certainly a very jealous one.   (*d*)

6 The real howl came when (a) a harmless madwoman
tried to stab George III; (b) George went mad; (c)
George got better; (d) George died.   (*c*) *b*

7 The Romantics (a) rivalled the eighteenth century in
their capacity for weeping, though their tears were
more refined; (b) wept in moderation; (c) still wept
a great deal, but uneasily because they had begun to
frown on masculine emotion; (d) were stoically dry-
eyed, because they felt crying was unmanly. (*c*)

8 In the end, Victorians believed that (a) only religious and poetic feelings should cause tears; (b) men
must work and women must weep; (c) no one
should weep; (d) only children should weep. (*b*)

9 Sobbing centuries have (a) been more numerous
than stoical ones; (b) been few and far between; (c)
generally happened under a queen; (d) been as numerous as the stoical ones.   (*a*)

10 The author's main intention is (a) to dispel a false
assumption about weeping; (b) to approve of men
weeping; (c) to disapprove of men weeping; (d) to
express the hope that men will weep again.   (*a*)

speed.....224.....w.p.m. (page 240) comprehension......... (page 235)

4:23

Comments

The first paragraph is not a mere introduction; it contains the
author's main proposition: the unwarranted nature of the
assumption that tears have always been effeminate; this paragraph must be read carefully. The answer to question 10 is not
that he himself approves or disapproves of weeping; nor the
hope – a personal observation – that we may yet weep again;
but his *purpose*, which is to dispel a false assumption about
weeping.

The author's purpose

The last exercise demonstrates how important it is to understand the author's purpose. Questions that should be in the
forefront of the reader's mind are: What is the author driving
at? What is he trying to show?

Exercise 4 (1150 words)

THE TROUBLE WITH PEOPLE

Extract from *The Hidden Persuaders** by Vance Packard

---

starting time 11:58.15

The trend in marketing to the depth approach was largely
impelled by difficulties the marketers kept encountering in trying to persuade people to buy all the products their companies
could fabricate.

One particularly disturbing difficulty was the apparent per-
versity and unpredictability of the prospective customers.
Marketers repeatedly suffered grievous losses in campaigns
that by all the rules of logic should have succeeded. The marketers felt increasing dissatisfaction with their conventional
methods for sizing up a market. These methods were known in
the trade most commonly as 'nose-counting'. Under nose-
counting, statistic-minded interviewers would determine the
percentage of married women, ages twenty-one to thirty-five,
in Omaha, Nebraska, who said they wanted, and would buy, a
three-legged stove if it cost no more than $249.

The trouble with this approach, they found, was that what
people might tell interviewers had only a remote bearing on
how the people would actually behave in a buying situation
when confronted with a three-legged stove or almost anything
else.

* © Vance Packard 1957. Reproduced by permission of Longmans,
Green & Co., Harlow, Essex, and of David McKay Co. Inc., New York.
The Hidden Persuaders is also available as a Pelican Book.

Gradually many perceptive marketers began becoming suspicious of three basic assumptions they had made, in their efforts to be logical, concerning the predictable behaviour of human beings, especially customers.

First, they decided, you can't assume that people know what they want.

A major ketchup maker kept getting complaints about its bottle, so it made a survey. Most of the people interviewed said they would prefer another type the company was considering. When the company went to the expense of bringing out this other bottle in test markets, it was overwhelmingly rejected in favour of the old bottle, even by people who had favoured it in interviews. In a survey of male beer drinkers the men expressed a strong preference for a 'nice dry beer'. When they were then asked how a beer could be dry they were stumped. Those who were able to offer any answers at all revealed widely different notions.

Second, some marketers concluded, you can't assume people will tell you the truth about their wants and dislikes even if they know them. What you are more likely to get, they decided, are answers that will protect the informants in their steadfast endeavour to appear to the world as really sensible, intelligent, rational beings. One management consulting firm has concluded that accepting the word of a customer as to what he wants is 'the least reliable index the manufacturer can have on what he ought to do to win customers'.

The Advertising Research Foundation took magazines to task for asking people what magazines they read frequently, and naïvely accepting the answers given as valid. The people, it contended, are likely to admit reading only magazines of high prestige value. One investigator suggests that if you seriously accepted people's answers you might assume that *Atlantic Monthly* is America's most-read magazine and some of the confession magazines the least read; whereas actually the confession magazines in question may have twenty times the readership of *Atlantic Monthly*.

A brewery making two kinds of beer made a survey to find what kind of people drank each beer, as a guide to its merchandisers. It asked people known to favour its general brand name: 'Do you drink light or the regular?' To its astonishment it found people reporting they drank light over the regular by better than three to one. The truth of the matter was that for years the company, to meet consumer demand, had been brewing nine times as much regular beer as light ale. It decided that in asking people that question it was in effect asking: Do you drink the kind preferred by people of refinement and discriminating taste, or do you just drink the regular stuff?

The Color Research Institute conducted an experiment after it began suspecting the reliability of people's comments. Women while waiting for a lecture had the choice of two waiting rooms. One was a functional modern chamber with gentle tones. It had been carefully designed for eye ease and to promote a relaxed feeling. The other room was a traditional room filled with period furniture, oriental rugs, expensive-looking wallpaper.

It was found that virtually all the women instinctively went into the Swedish modern room to do their waiting. Only when every chair was filled did the women start to overflow into the more ornate room. After the lecture the ladies were asked, 'Which of those two rooms do you like the better?' They looked thoughtfully at the two rooms, and then eighty-four per cent of them said the period room was the nicer room. . . .

Finally, the marketers decided it is dangerous to assume that people can be trusted to behave in a rational way.

The Color Research Institute had what it felt was a startling encounter with this proneness to irrationality when it tested package designs for a new detergent. It was testing to see if a woman is influenced more than she realizes, in her opinion of a product, by the package. It gave the housewives three different boxes filled with detergent and requested that they try them all out for a few weeks and then report which was the best for delicate clothing. The wives were given the impression that they had been given three different types of detergent. Actually only the boxes were different; the detergents inside were identical.

The design for one was predominantly yellow. The yellow in

41

the test was used because some merchandisers were convinced that yellow was the best colour for store shelves because it has very strong visual impact. Another box was predominantly blue without any yellow in it; and the third box was blue but with splashes of yellow.

In their reports the housewives stated that the detergent in the brilliant yellow box was too strong; it even allegedly ruined their clothes in some cases. As for the detergent in the predominantly blue box, the wives complained in many cases that it left their clothes dirty looking. The third box, which contained what the institute felt was an ideal balance of colours in the package design, overwhelmingly received favourable responses. The women used such words as 'fine' and 'wonderful' in describing the effect the detergent in that box had on their clothes.

A department store that had become sceptical of the rationality of its customers tried an experiment. One of its slowest-moving items was priced at fourteen cents. It changed the price to two for twenty-nine cents. Sales promptly increased thirty per cent when the item was offered at this 'bargain' price. . . .

Business Week, in commenting on the often seemingly irrational behaviour of consumers, said: 'People don't seem to be reasonable.' However, it made this further point: 'But people do act with purpose. Their behaviour makes sense if you think about it in terms of its goals, of people's needs and their motives. That seems to be the secret of understanding or manipulating people.'

---

finishing time 11:58:30

QUESTIONS

1 The difficulty facing marketers was that prospective customers were (a) mistrustful; (b) inarticulate; (c) secretive; (d) seemingly perverse and unpredictable. (d)

2 'Nose-counting' was (a) unreliable, because the

method of sampling was defective; (b) unsound, because the questions were invariably 'loaded'; (c) right in principle; (d) found to provide information that had only a remote bearing on how people actually behaved.　　　　　　　　　　(d)

3　The conclusion of many marketers, supported in the article by evidence from the consumers of ketchup and 'nice dry beer', was that it could *not* be assumed that customers (a) knew what they wanted; (b) did not change their preferences overnight; (c) were influenced by quality and style; (d) were highly susceptible to persuasive advertising.　　　　(a)

4　Another conclusion of some marketers, supported in the article by evidence from readers of magazines and consumers of light beer and regular beer, was that people (a) purchased more of what they thought had prestige value; (b) did not always tell the truth; (c) were surprisingly truthful; (d) said whatever they imagined would please.　　　(b)

5　When the Color Research Institute questioned women about two waiting-rooms that had been provided for them, their replies showed that the majority (a) had marked preferences; (b) had no preference either way; (c) did not act in accordance with their stated preference; (d) could not make up their minds.　　　　　　　　　　　(c)

6　We can infer from the testing of package designs for a new detergent that (a) customers can be influenced by a scientific approach to design; (b) package design is not as important as it was thought to be; (c) design influences some people much more than others; (d) attitudes to package design are unpredictable.　　　　　　　　　(d) a

7　A third conclusion was that it was dangerous to assume that (a) motives are simple; (b) motives do not conflict; (c) people do not have unconscious motives; (d) people can be trusted to behave in a rational way.　　　　　　　　　　(d)

8   The experiment of re-pricing the slowest-moving
    article in a department store is some indication that
    the average American (a) goes for what he is offered
    as a bargain, whether it is or not; (b) is unusually
    discriminating about prices; (c) puts price before
    quality; (d) is gullible enough to assume that price
    governs quality.   (a)

9   A comment of *Business Week* was that people (a)
    seem to be reasonable, but behave unreasonably; (b)
    don't seem to be reasonable, but do act with pur-
    pose; (c) are reasonable, but it is difficult, and some-
    times impossible, to get at their reasons; (d) fluc-
    tuate between reason and emotion.   (b)

10 *Business Week* concludes that (a) behaviour is diffi-
    cult to predict, because motives are largely uncon-
    scious; (b) as people are emotional they must be
    understood or manipulated through their emotions;
    (c) behaviour makes sense in terms of goals, needs,
    and motives; (d) people can be persuaded up to a
    point, but they cannot be manipulated.   (b)c

---

speed........w.p.m. (page 240) comprehension........ (page 235)

Comments

The author states the problem and the circumstances giving rise
to the problem. He then tells us his purpose: to explain the
suspicions of many perceptive marketers about 'three basic
assumptions' they had made – here we read carefully, as we do
when their views are made known, boldly announced by the
words: 'First', 'Second', and 'Finally'. When there is a problem
we can expect a conclusion: this is given in the quotations
from *Business Week*, which require very careful reading. The
evidence of the marketers can be read at speed, provided their
three assertions have been clearly understood.

Suggestions for Practice

The art of quick comprehension is to get the right amount and the right kind of information from the page. A good way to practise is to read for a *general* comprehension.

1. Choose several fairly short and easy passages. Do not calculate your speed. Read for the main points; jot them down; and check your comprehension.

2. *From now on review your comprehension of all practice material in relation to the way in which you have read it.*

CHAPTER 3

READING AS A DIGESTIVE PROCESS

Selection and Organization

THE reader is not a passive recipient, like a container or a sponge. This sounds trite, but until quite modern times, authoritarian, jug-and-bottle methods of teaching were the rule and the tradition dies hard. The most self-respecting, self-propelling person, turned reader, can give his mind some rough treatment that would shock him if he knew what he was doing.

The mind, whatever else it may be, is a universe of relationships. Understanding is the ability to see relevant relationships. The mind is not a collection of discrete items, like buttons in a box. The reader *relates* what he reads to what he already knows. 'Taking things in' is a process *of* the mind, not an injection *into* the mind.

There is a close analogy between the work of the mind and that of the digestive system. The proper food of the mind is relationships: items grouped in 'wholes' – patterns of thought, which, for want of a better word, we shall call schemas. Schemas make sense and are digestible. Unrelated details are highly indigestible and may require endless mastication, hence the prevalence of mnemonics, which are substitutes for schemas.

In all activity we have to ignore most of the countless impressions that bombard our senses – we live by cues. The reader creates schemas by *selecting* what is relevant. The purpose of reading is to obtain a 'digest' of schemas, a pattern of thought.

The mental system, like the physical system, can digest so much at a time, and no more. Complicated ideas give the mind more work than simple ideas, and, because of the limitations of the mental digestive system, require slower reading. Specific details that the reader needs to remember, but which do not fit into a pattern, also require slow reading.

On the other hand, if the reader is familiar with the subject he may be able to read quite fast, even when the information is complicated or detailed, because he is able to relate it to his own pattern of thought – he has less work to do. When readers start experimenting with speeds, they may read a passage much too fast or much too slowly, and find they have missed the essential meaning. Reading that is unduly fast gives the mind too much work in too short a time. Reading that is unduly slow is liable to put a strain on the system by feeding it a heavy diet of unnecessary details and small ideas, even mere words, so that the reading time, though long, is not long enough, and the vital work of selecting and organizing is neglected or left undone.

Readers sometimes find that when they have reached the end of a passage they have forgotten the beginning: earlier information seems to have been pushed out by later information. What happens is that the earlier material is not sufficiently digested in the time available, the mind withdraws its energy to cope with new demands, and the half-digested information, which has no schemas to hold it in the mind, is easily forgotten. Two principles emerge from this concept of reading as a digestive process:

1. Learning by Understanding

The reader must assimilate – LEARN – *by understanding and not by memorizing.* Learning by memorizing is only appropriate when there are unrelated items, which in general reading are few and far between. The essence of memorizing is repetition but the slowest reading is inadequate for this; and even if it were possible to memorize the text, this would not in itself lead to understanding. Learning by understanding is selective, discriminating, and organizing; memorizing is inclusive, undiscriminating, and repetitive.

2. Flexibility

As there is a limit to the amount of information that can be digested in a given time, the reader must vary his speed of reading. When the meaning is difficult he must take more time by reading more slowly; when the meaning is easy he needs less time and can read faster.

In Part II we shall extend this principle of flexibility. In order to provide time for the digestive process the reader may, for example, skim through an article for the framework; then read quickly for general information; follow this by reading selected parts quite slowly; and finally, perhaps, skim over the text to locate a few specific items that can only be learnt by memorizing. In this way he proceeds from the general to the particular and is able to relate the new information in progressive stages to his existing knowledge; furthermore, there is a constructive repetition quite unlike the repetition involved in memorizing. By distributing his time and effort he saves time and increases his efficiency.

The skills that are the subject of this book should all be considered in terms of reading as a digestive process.

A Note on Digests

Readers put this kind of question: 'Why don't writers write the way we are asked to read?' Our previous observation that the reader has to make a mental digest is no apology for literary digests. If a brief statement is necessary it should be written specially for the purpose; a digest is too often an unbalanced abbreviation by an intermediary of something that has been written for a totally different purpose.

Students we have tested on the reading of digests have as a rule not retained the information as long as those who, by reading the originals, have been obliged to look *for* their knowledge; nor have they comprehended so well: some have had only a superficial understanding, as though they had looked *at* the material.

The author must give the reader time to assimilate; if there were no amplification or illustration, no constructive repetition or variation, the material would remain undigested. It is never our intention, therefore, to imply that incidental material is unnecessary, something to which the efficient reader turns a blind eye. The incidentals are there because they contribute to understanding, arouse interest, stimulate the imagination and give the reader a chance to use his own knowledge; they also provide the colour and tone that are often the best indication of the author's intention and purpose. Our argument is that the reader should not spend a *disproportionate* amount of time on things he can grasp easily; that because there is a limit to what he can digest in a given time he must vary his speed of reading according to the nature of the material. Flexibility implies activity. Pre-digested material, by precluding this activity, is not good food for thought.

What to Do Next

Find the average of your speeds for the last two passages, and the average of your comprehension scores. Take these as your standard when reading the next two passages.

1. *Below 250 w.p.m.* Concentrate on the main statements, but move briskly through the illustrations.

2. *Between 250 and 350 w.p.m.* Aim at flexibility – there is scope for this in the next two passages. If your comprehension is below 6, then you must be prepared to slow down; but do so by concentrating on the main points, which will increase your flexibility; if you slow down uniformly your speed may suffer unduly.

3. *Over 350 w.p.m.* Go steadily and do not sacrifice your comprehension to speed; be content with small gains. If your comprehension is below 7, then slow down by reading more attentively when confronted with the main points or with new information.

Previewing

In the next two exercises, glance over the passage for 10 seconds. *Count this as part of your reading time.* We suggest you glance at the first line or two of each paragraph and the last few lines of the passage, taking in the words and phrases that strike you, without any attempt at close reading. You may obtain little more than an expansion of the title, but this will be quite enough to start you thinking ahead. Do not start reading as soon as you have finished this previewing, but allow yourself a few minutes to collect your thoughts and think about the topic.

This 'anticipation' is a basic skill of reading and one that can be improved quickly and easily. We do not wish to say much about it at this stage: we prefer you to experiment for yourself.

Reading

The next two passages, the first on the psychology of writing and reading, the second on flats versus houses, are exercises in relating your own knowledge to what is given in the text: we have just been considering the psychology of reading; and there is little factual information in the passage on flats versus houses with which you are not perfectly familiar.

Comprehension

These two passages have questions which you answer in your own words. The answers in the Key should be taken as a guide; if the wording of the answers keeps fairly close to the text, this is to facilitate checking.

Exercise 5   (880 words)

LOOK AT A THREEPENNY-PIECE
Extract from *Teach Yourself to Study** by G. G. Neill-Wright

---

starting time

Look at a threepenny-piece. You are aware at once of the flat sides, the colour of the metal, the three thrift flowers, the inscription, and the date. You are aware at the same time of the relations between these – aware that the inscription is round two-thirds of the circumference, above and to the sides of the flowers, that the date is underneath, and so on. Your

* Reproduced by permission of the author and the English Universities Press.

attention passes as freely from the flowers to the sides, or to the date, as to the description of the colour. This is much more like our three-dimensional structure than like the chain or even the plane figure. Why do we ever take the chain as our model in learning? Why do we try to set out the items of our experience in single file?

There is a simple explanation. What is communicated from one mind to another is communicated mainly in words, and words, whether spoken or printed, must be set out in a row. Thus communication does violence to the complexities and intricacies of our thoughts. The speaker or writer is put to the trouble of forcing his complex and many-sided matter into a simple straight line; what he perceives or grasps in one comprehensive mental act must be dissected and rearranged like a square linen sheet cut into strips to make a rope. Thus, to go back to the threepenny-piece, the inscription, the flowers, the date, the relation of the inscription to the flowers, the relation of the date to the flowers, and so on, must all be separately mentioned one after the other, instead of being grasped simultaneously; and they must be set out in one particular order, though any other order may be equally appropriate. The hearer, or reader, must then take this sequence of bits and pieces and put its elements together for himself, so as to re-create in his own mind the complex pattern, with its many inter-relations between the items, to which the linear arrangement has done violence.

What we learn for ourselves from our practical experience is not arranged in our minds chain fashion. The farmer knows his fields and woods this way and that, so that he can cross from one point to another without stopping to think how he must go; and he can go back and forward in time in thinking of rotation of crops, past and future, draining done or to be done, successive accretions of buildings, houses and cottages and barns. The engineer has the different parts of his engine simultaneously in mind when he is trying to locate some fault: he does not have to follow the order of topics adopted in some text-book. Knowledge for use does not have a linear arrangement in the memory. It is only when knowledge has to be communicated that it must move like an army on the march in column of route – a formation which has no military value except as a means of passing from one area of deployment to another.

The art of writing is largely the art of imposing this linear order upon more or less recalcitrant material. The art of reading is largely the reconstruction of a multi-dimensional structure from a linear one. A good writer presents his material so as to facilitate this reconstruction. . . .

There is an analogy in the mechanical process by which the scanning apparatus used in television breaks up the picture into a temporal succession of varying brightnesses, and the receiving apparatus presents these with an appearance of simultaneity. The more work an author puts into his writing, the more likely he is to perform a similar miracle in the mind of his reader. . . . But one-half of the miracle is worked by the mind of the reader.

The art of study, when it is directed to printed material, is largely the art of reconstructing in one's own mind the pictures, thoughts or emotion patterns which the writer has sought to convey through the medium of words. To do this we must grasp each unit as a whole and understand the complex and intricate ways in which all its parts are inter-related: it is not enough to direct attention to the order in which they are set out and seek to retain them as a chain of linear associations. This may sound formidable. It is not really so. It is what we do spontaneously with any material which commands our interest – a novel, an anecdote, a cinema film or the description of a machine or other structure connected with our daily activities or hobbies. Interest means more than this power of reconstruction, for it involves also a motive for using it. Both must be present, if what is being studied is to be grasped and retained.

The student's conscious aim is probably to remember what he reads. This is an endeavour which frequently defeats his own ends, for to aim at remembering something comes very near to being afraid that we shall forget it, and such fears have a nasty habit of ensuring their own justification. The student's aim should rather be to understand what he reads, for what we understand and are interested in is likely to stick to us.

---

finishing time

QUESTIONS

1 What does the author show by his example of the three-penny piece?
2 What is the speaker or writer obliged to do to communicate his knowledge?
3 What is the hearer or reader obliged to do in order to comprehend?
4 What does the author explain by the analogy of the television set?
5 Why is study not so formidable as it sounds?
6 Why is it that the student's conscious effort to remember often defeats its own ends?
7 What should be the student's aim when he is reading?

---

speed.........w.p.m. (page 240) comprehension.........(page 237)

Comments

The author begins with an illustration to show that we perceive things in their relationships: the theme of the present chapter, which will have found an echo in your reading. He then explains how ideas that are *communicated* from one mind to another must be set out in a row, chain fashion. The hearer or reader must recreate the whole – the pattern of schemas – from the linear arrangements of the words. This is the essence of the psychology of communication between author and reader, and is the foundation of Part II of this book.

Exercise 6 (940 words)

FLATS VERSUS HOUSES

Extract from *Applied Geography** by L. Dudley Stamp

---

starting time

Britain almost more than any other country in the world must seriously face the problem of building upwards: that is to say of accommodating a considerable proportion of its population in high blocks of flats. It is said that the Englishman is averse to this type of existence, but, if the case is such, he does in fact differ from the inhabitants of most countries of the world today. In the past our own blocks of flats have been associated with the lower-income groups and they have lacked the obvious amenities, such as central heating, constant hot-water supply, electrically operated lifts from top to bottom, and so on, as well as such details, important notwithstanding, as easy facilities for disposal of dust and rubbish and storage places for prams on the ground floor, playgrounds for children on the top of the buildings, and drying grounds for washing. It is likely that the controversy regarding flats versus individual houses will continue to rage for a long time as far as Britain is concerned. And it is unfortunate that there should be hot feelings on both sides whenever this subject is raised. Those who oppose the building of flats base their case primarily on the presumption that everyone prefers an individual home and garden and on the high cost per unit of accommodation. The latter ignores the higher cost of providing full services to a scattered community and the cost in both money and time of the journeys to work for the suburban dweller.

A compromise would seem to be obvious. Surely a person in the course of life is likely to live in at least four homes, which may be of somewhat different types. There is in the first instance the home in which one's parents live, in which one perhaps is born, and lives one's childhood. One has as a rule

* © L. Dudley Stamp, 1960, 1961, 1963, Pelican Books. Reproduced by permission of the author.

no greater degree of choice over this than one has over the choice of one's parents. It is in the later teenages that the desire for independence grows quite naturally, the student at College, whether male or female, develops naturally a desire to live a life of his or her own, and searches for that which is virtually unobtainable in most of the cities of Britain, a tiny self-contained flat of a couple of rooms at the most – a bedroom, a sitting-room-study, with a bathroom and small kitchen. Quite frequently there comes the stage when two students will share such quarters, or when the idea grows that two can live as cheaply as one, and the young husband and wife – perhaps, both studying, both working – want accommodation very much of this character. They certainly have no desire at that stage for a larger house with the responsibilities of a garden, nor does the wife wish to be separated from the job which she has undertaken or her studies – the great desire of both partners is to be as near as possible to the daily occupation, and especially to be near the centre of the town, where may be found so many of the amenities desired in youth and early manhood – the cinema, the live theatre, perhaps art galleries, and concert halls and library, college, or night school. Unfortunately many students are compelled to waste an immense amount of time in getting to their work; one sees them strap-hanging in the tube, trying to study at the same time. Surely this could be obviated by building blocks of flats especially for young people near their work.

Many others would if they could live near their work. Take those who are concerned with the running of London's hotels and restaurants, theatres and cinemas, who cannot finish work until late at night. What a joy to be able, as it were, to tumble into bed, without the necessity of worrying about last trains home. It would seem that a compromise in all cases is to build blocks of flats near the centre of the town so that those who wish could live in them and be near their work or pleasure, as the case may be.

The third stage, requiring the third type of accommodation, comes rather naturally with the arrival of the family. The wife gives up her job, devotes her life to the occupation of motherhood, when for the benefit of the children's health space and fresh air are desirable. At this stage in life there is so much to be said for the garden, where the husband coming home during the week-end can himself gain advantages to health and strength by working about the house or garden. The separate or semi-detached dwelling, with its own garden, belongs especially to this stage. But a fourth stage arrives, when the children grow up and leave the home, get married, and the elderly couple have no longer the strength to look after the garden, no longer the interest; when creature comforts mean very much. Some still opt for the peace and quiet of a tiny country cottage, and they play an important part in maintaining the social structure of rural life. Others gravitate back to a town flat or maisonette, with such advantages as constant hot water, central heating, and electric lifts and refrigerators, there to enjoy that which they have missed earlier in life in concerts, lectures, and other intellectual fare which only a city can provide. Again the need is for the two- or three-roomed, comfortably arranged flat. If one only thought in terms of getting the right proportion of these four or five types of home, surely our planning would be better.

---

finishing time

QUESTIONS

1 In the past, blocks of flats in this country have been associated with the lower-income groups. What other point is made in this connexion?

2 What are the two main arguments of those who oppose the building of flats?

3 What two facts are ignored by those who are opposed to flats?

4 (a) Who need flats of one kind or another?
   (b) Who need houses?

5 What is the author's final conclusion?

---

speed.........w.p.m. (page 240) comprehension.........(page 237)

Comments

This passage can be read quite fast because the subject matter is common knowledge. We have found, however, that familiarity with the contents is no guarantee that the reading will be any faster than usual. Articles of this kind are sometimes poorly comprehended; it may be that familiarity leads to inflexible reading, insufficient time being given to the leading ideas. This particular article, moreover, has another difficulty for the unwary, inflexible reader: it starts with a problem and reaches a conclusion, which is stated very briefly. In our experience, readers are inclined to neglect conclusions; perhaps because there is a natural tendency to speed up as the end of the article – the target – is approached.

Here, the author states the problem – building upwards; and follows this with a preliminary discussion of the assumptions of those who are opposed to the building of flats. He then analyses the situation: four stages of life, requiring at least four different kinds of home; and, from this, arrives at his conclusion – the right proportion of these types of home.

There are three things to note:

1. When there is a problem, be on the alert for the conclusion.

2. When the discussion of a problem is divided into parts or stages, there may be a preamble explaining how the material is organized; this kind of information always merits careful attention. In this article the author makes things easy by anticipating his conclusion: 'A compromise would seem to be obvious'; and by giving an outline of the stages of his discussion: 'at least four homes ... of different types'.

3. It is not unusual for an author to draw attention to the parts or stages of his discussion. This article gives appropriate indications: 'In the first instance'; 'the third stage'; 'a fourth stage'; but there is no formal announcement of the second stage.

Suggestions for Practice

Continue to practise as we have recommended in page 45.

CHAPTER 4

CONCENTRATION AND EFFORT

How to concentrate and how to improve memory are the topics on which we receive most questions. There is a very close connexion between concentration (or attention) and memory; and our approach is similar to the one we adopt for memory (Chapter 10).

The Requirements of Good Concentration

1. *A motive*

If the reader is clear about his purpose, he has a motive for reading and finds it easier to concentrate. The reader who takes everything as it comes, who reads and never asks why he is reading, often finds it difficult to concentrate: he has no major target; his reading lacks drive.

2. *An interest*

As the reader's interests develop, they acquire specialized digestive systems that make concentration easier; he is therefore able to concentrate on some things better than others, according to the degree of interest. The inability to concentrate on a particular topic usually means that there is no digestive system capable of dealing with it adequately; and little interest. The *will* to learn cannot compensate for a lack of interest.

3. *An intention to concentrate*

This gives the reader a mental 'set' (On your marks. Get *set*.) which excludes distractions.

The reader, through a sense of urgency or because he is daunted by the task, may over-concentrate and exclude thinking – the active part of reading – along with distracting thoughts.

The intention to concentrate is not enough; the reader, as we shall now see, must do the things that make concentration possible: read actively, read for the meaning behind the words, and use his existing knowledge.

4. *Active reading*

The reader must think for himself and not expect the author to think for him. To concentrate properly he should be as active and spontaneous as he is in conversation or discussion. Somewhat in these terms, as if he were saying: 'I agree'; 'That's obvious'; 'I see your point, but I don't agree'; 'Why don't you give an example?' 'Now I see what you're driving at.' There is a responsive mood, not, of course, a running commentary.

In the exercises the reader is only tested for comprehension; but if he is to concentrate well, he must read actively; which means that his critical faculties cannot be kept in abeyance. Criticism, however, if the attention is not to wander, should be within the movement of the author's thought.

5. *Reading for the meaning behind the words*

This is the right method: learning by understanding. Words must be understood in their context. The reader who assimilates meaning, rather than words, usually has no difficulty in concentrating, because he can retain the ideas in his own language; he has command of the context. If, however, he allows the ideas to remain too closely associated with the author's actual wording, he may find it difficult to concentrate, because when the words are forgotten, the meaning becomes elusive. If he absorbs mere words, he is unlikely to understand anything; all he does is concentrate on concentrating.

Here is an example of what happens when one concentrates on words. A friend attended a meeting in a room where there was a lot of noise from passing traffic. He said afterwards that although he could hear the speaker, he had to concentrate so hard on the actual words that he found it almost impossible to follow the meaning.

6. *Using one's existing knowledge*

When the reader uses his own knowledge he casts a network of schemas round the new information; which makes concentration easier. Reading actively, reading for the meaning behind the words, and using one's existing knowledge are aspects of the relating process of comprehension. A good way of concentrating is to stimulate this relating process by trying to *anticipate* the author's approach before starting to read; the reader who uses his existing knowledge by thinking about the topic in advance is much more likely to go on thinking for himself while he is reading. Anticipation is a major skill. We shall say a little about it when we come to the following exercises; and make it the subject of Chapter 7.

7. *A challenge*

If the reader is to concentrate, he needs the challenge of new interests, different points of view, and information that makes demands on his understanding; without this challenge his attention is liable to wander. His goals, however, should not be too far in advance of his attainments; aiming too high can have disastrous consequences.

Efficiency is itself a challenge. Even when the material is not particularly interesting, good methods, ways of disposing of the project as quickly and as easily as possible, can provide a most effective stimulus to concentration.

In the early stages of training, the reader should practise on material that is fairly easy, concentrating on the method of reading, which is the real challenge; he can then extend himself by degrees; and at a later stage try more difficult assignments, always remembering what we have said about goals and attainments.

Distribution of Effort

Efficiency is not commensurate with effort but with the way it is distributed. As the reader can only digest so much at a time, he must read flexibly, varying his speed and applying his effort where it is most needed.

We were struck by the fact that when readers joined our courses late and had to read long passages as their first exercise, their speeds were often particularly slow. We therefore tested students, giving them a fairly easy long passage and a more difficult short one; most of them read the long passage at a much slower speed. The students' summaries of the long passages often showed a preoccupation with the actual wording of the text and an attempt to assimilate more information than was possible in a single reading; their effort was not properly distributed. We are inclined to think that the evidence for the speed of the average reader – based on the reading of short passages – is out of touch with reality; and that readers in general are less efficient than the tests indicate. We get the same impression when we question people about the time they take to read books. Yet with practice, people are able to read long passages more easily than short ones, when they have the knack of distributing their effort, because long passages offer more scope for flexible reading.

We shall see in Part II that often the best way to distribute effort is to space it: reading a long passage several times at different speeds, for example, may not infrequently save both time and effort.

Fatigue

Wasted effort contributes to fatigue; but however efficient the reader is, he cannot apply his effort indefinitely without fatigue. Very little is known about fatigue in reading; and it is almost impossible to generalize on account of the complications of motive and interest. Nevertheless, reading is not always of absorbing interest; and the following points are worth considering:

1. The volume and rhythm of reading

There is a limit to what the reader can cope with in the course of the day. Longer hours do not necessarily increase the amount of information that is assimilated and may even reduce it, because there is unconscious resistance to excessive effort; shorter hours may conceivably increase efficiency and the total volume of reading.

Readers have individual rhythms. It seems, however, that favourable times for mental work are in the morning, before the body is fully active, and during the evening, when it is relaxed and not too tired, rather than in the afternoon when it reaches a peak of activity.

2. *Effort and fatigue*

Fatigue slows down the reader's mental digestive system; this is why excessive fatigue impairs comprehension. Readers can have too much of a good thing and get bored; if this happens, effort is consumed keeping the mind at work, when the inclination is to do something else.

Excessive and sustained fatigue may even tire the lower centre of the brain, which controls a reserve of energy; the effect is a sudden outpouring of uncoordinated energy. (The athlete's 'second wind' is an example of this.)

3. *Resting*

A useful tip may be gained from industrial psychology, where the principle of 'rest pauses' is to rest when one is *not* tired – ideally just before the onset of fatigue – so that one does not get tired, or not so quickly. The reader's pauses should be fairly brief; otherwise there is a wasteful process of warming up. Voluntary rests are more beneficial than the involuntary ones the reader takes surreptitiously.

A change is often as good as a rest; this is why some readers keep several books going at once. A complete change is advisable; otherwise it may be difficult to keep the ideas apart and one subject may confuse the other.

A Note on Vocalization and Inner Speech

Vocalization is mouthing the words while reading; or using the vocal muscles without making any sound. Inner speech is hearing the unvoiced sounds of the words. Vocalizing is an unnecessary and detrimental habit and should be avoided. In the enthusiasm to 'break the sound barrier' readers are often warned against inner speech; and as most readers seem to hear snatches of words, this could be a matter of general concern. In our opinion this warning is ill-considered.

Vocalization

The reader who vocalizes is concentrating on the actual words and unconsciously trying to remember them; vocalizing helps the process of memorizing, and readers who do not normally voice the words often do so when they are in difficulties. As we have seen, memorizing makes quick comprehension difficult, if not impossible. The remedy is to read actively, so as not to become preoccupied with the words as such.

Various devices have been recommended for breaking the habit directly. One method is to read with a pencil in the mouth, like a bit; but this cannot prevent muscular activity in the throat. Another method is to recite the alphabet while reading, in order to break the association between the printed word and its sound; but we fail to see how anyone can read actively if he is reciting the alphabet: he is likely to pay even more attention to the words themselves.

There is a popular assumption that readers who vocalize cannot read faster than they speak, about 180 w.p.m.; but experiments have shown that some readers are capable of vocalizing at over 400 w.p.m.; and we ourselves were amazed to find we could make recognizable sounds, without practice, at 360 w.p.m. In actual fact, vocalizers rarely exceed the speed at which they speak; but this is not because they cannot vocalize faster, but because they are trying to remember the words.

The reader who voices the words can only rid himself of the habit by reading actively.

Inner Speech

It is too often assumed that the unvoiced sounds of words should also be eliminated or, at any rate, reduced to a minimum. If inner speech occurs because the reader is merely repeating the author's words, then something is radically wrong. The remedy, again, is active reading. If inner speech is the accompaniment of the reader's own activity, we can see nothing whatever against it.

William James suggested that when thinking became difficult, it was supported by imagery, like a bird hopping from bough to bough: the boughs being the images, and the flight of the bird the 'imageless thought': the swifter the thought, the fewer the images. Controversy raged round this topic for years and was abortive. *Some* imagery accompanies thought; but how, when, where, or why is a mystery.

Some people have powerful visual imagery; and as there is convincing evidence that those who are good in one kind of imagery tend to be good in other kinds as well, some readers may find that good visual imagery and inner speech go together. The amount of inner speech there is depends on the reader's mental constitution. If he reads actively, he has nothing to fear.

Occasionally, readers say that as soon as they try to read our exercises faster they hear every word of the text as clearly as if they were listening to a gramophone record. What seems to happen is that they have recourse to *speeding*, in all probability at a uniform rate, and consequently the time they give to the more important ideas is inadequate. Failing to comprehend, they resort to memorizing, which makes matters worse; but as the best way to memorize is to have as many different sensory impressions as possible, they vocalize and speak the words inwardly. As soon as they stop speeding they no longer attempt to memorize and the clamour ceases.

We are surprised that so much stress is laid on this subject: one would think that vocalizing was universal among slow readers; which is certainly not the case. It is possible that methods of training which emphasize speed may themselves be a cause of vocalizing and inner speech.

What to Do Next

Previewing

In the next two exercises, extend your previewing to 20 seconds. *Count this as part of your reading time.*

Reading

Exercise 7 contains some tables of figures; in consulting them, let yourself be guided by the text. With good anticipation Exercise 8 can be read fast; aim at a general understanding and make no attempt to remember precise details.

Comprehension

Exercise 7 has six free-answer questions and four multiple-choice questions. Exercise 8 has seven free-answer questions and three multiple-choice questions.

Exercise 7 (1200 words)

THE DRIVER AND OTHER ROAD USERS

Extract from *Road Traffic Accidents** by L. G. Norman

---

starting time

The road user carries much of the responsibility for traffic accidents: the vehicle driver for the safety of others as well as himself, the pedestrian mainly for his own safety, while the passenger carries relatively little responsibility. The consumption of alcohol before going on the roads increases the incidence of accidents among all categories of adult road user; this important problem is dealt with in the next chapter.

Driving is a skill which requires training, and, like other skills, it can be maintained at a high level only by regular practice. The time usually required to train a London bus driver who has never driven before is 50 hours at the wheel, spread over at least four weeks. The average private car driver receives considerably less training than this before he drives on his own and proceeds to acquire experience. As has been shown, increasing experience is a major factor in accident reduction, for inexperienced drivers have high accident rates. Experience cannot be taught, but it can be guided. Studies of

Public Health Papers No. 12. Reproduced by permission of the World Health Organization.

training methods for motor vehicle drivers have not been undertaken, but the inculcation of 'defensive' driving techniques is important. It may be that 'good', i.e., safe, drivers anticipate or in some other way avoid pre-accident situations.

The psychological problem in road safety is essentially one of vigilance. Vigilance is affected by environmental conditions; a practical application of vigilance studies lies in the teaching of anticipation, a very important quality for driving. The ease with which a driver's attention is diverted is important but difficult to measure. It is difficult to determine the degree to which a driver is absorbed in his driving by measuring his overt responses directly, but the spare mental capacity of drivers in a subsidiary task, such as an oral arithmetic test, can be measured. It is possible that a driver's behaviour could be adversely affected in this way, for example, by the use of a radio to listen to important or interesting information when he should be paying full attention to the road. No evidence is yet available, however, on the relationship, if any, between the use of car radios and road accidents. This is an illustration of how much needs to be done and of how little scientific methods have been applied to study the consequences of scientific development.

The average probable occurrences encountered while driving have been suggested by Platt (1958) to be as follows:

Observations	..	200 per mile
Decisions	.. ..	20 per mile
Errors	.. .. ..	1 per 2 miles
Near-collisions	..	1 per 500 miles
Collisions	.. ..	1 per 61 000 miles
Personal injuries	..	1 per 430 000 miles
Fatal accidents	..	1 per 16 000,000 miles

The frequency of the first four of these events was based on general observations; of the last three, on published statistics.

Personal and emotional adjustments offer a more promising field of study of accident causation. The proposition that 'a man drives as he lives' was originally put forward by Tillman and Hobbs (1949). They found that a high-accident group of taxi drivers contrasted with a low-accident group in showing marked intolerance for authority, aggression, an unstable home background and various aspects of antisocial behaviour. This lends support to the view that the personal characteristics of road users exert a considerable influence on accident rates.

Table 16. Death Rates per 100,000 Population from Motor Vehicle Accidents, by Age, Sex, and Marital Status, United States, Average 1949-51

Age and Sex		Single	Married	Widowed	Divorced
20–24	M	74	46	140	157
	F	13	9	55	43
25–34	M	62	32	146	134
	F	11	8	26	24
35–44	M	49	28	88	97
	F	7	8	20	22
45–54	M	51	29	68	93
	F	8	10	16	18
55–59	M	63	33	70	91
	F	10	13	16	19
60–64	M	70	37	75	109
	F	14	16	19	28
65–69	M	79	43	80	118
	F	17	18	19	23
70–74	M	98	49	91	150
	F	23	23	21	41
75 and over	M	121	65	98	199
	F	34	24	24	53

A further example of the effect of 'way of life' upon road traffic accident rates is given in Table 16, which shows a considerable variation at all ages in road accident mortality rates according to marital status. These rates are derived from a population basis, and the true exposure to risk in terms of mileage driven is unknown; caution in their interpretation is therefore necessary. Also, the relation between marital status and accidents may not be a direct one. For males, married men have the lowest rates, the rates increasing through the single and widowed until the highest rates are reached in the divorced group, which has a mortality about three times as high as the married. Differences for women are similar, but less marked at the higher ages.

Greater emotional instability has been found in a group of drivers who experienced repeated road traffic accidents compared with accident-free drivers. This could be cause and effect; it may be that in drivers who have repeated accidents, the accidents are but one expression of a faulty adjustment to the demands of life. This may appear as a desire for dangerous living; some people probably have more courage and less fear of death or injury than others. The view has also been expressed that many accidents are unconsciously motivated and serve certain personal needs; this view has not been tested in relation to road traffic accidents. The theory that 'a man drives as he lives' may also apply to pedestrians: an aggressive person with marked intolerance for authority and many antisocial characteristics seems likely, on the face of it, to make an unsafe pedestrian, but this hypothesis has not been tested.

An anlysis of the neuropsychological qualities used in driving and of the way in which they are applied to the driving task was undertaken by Ventra (1960), but few laboratory or experimental studies of the nature of the driving task have yet been undertaken. Emphasis is often placed on tests of reaction time in relation to accident prevention, but safe driving does not depend solely on quickness of reaction. At first sight it would appear that drivers with the shortest reaction times should be able to act most promptly in the moments preceding an accident and should therefore have fewer accidents than more slowly reacting drivers. That this idea may be misleading is suggested by the fact that drivers aged 18–25, who have the fastest reaction times, experience more accidents than middle-aged drivers. Young drivers give a better performance on psychomotor tests generally. It appears that as a man ages in the middle range, his reactions are slower, his hearing diminshes, his eye–hand co-ordination deteriorates – *but he becomes a safe driver*. This increased safety is probably due to experience which results in the avoidance of accident situations, a quality which appears to be better developed in the middle-aged than in the young. Avoidance of the accident situation depends on the degree of care exercised, on experience, on the important quality of anticipation, and perhaps on other factors as yet unrecognized.

finishing time

QUESTIONS

1 What is necessary if the skill of driving is to be maintained at a high level?

2 What obvious deficiency is there in the training of the private car driver?

3 What is thought to be the main quality of the good, safe driver?

4 What essentially is the psychological problem in road safety?

5 The car radio (a) causes accidents by distracting the driver's attention; (b) may possibly have an adverse effect on driving; (c) has no connexion whatever with road accidents; (d) helps drivers to relax and therefore reduces frustration.

6 In the table of average probable occurrences encountered while driving, the figure for errors is (a) 1 per 2 miles; (b) 1 per 50 miles; (c) 1 per 100 miles; (d) 1 per 200 miles.

7 The investigation into the accident rate of taxi drivers (a) lends support to the theory that the personal characteristics of drivers exert a considerable influence on accident rates; (b) is conclusive evidence that a man drives as he lives; (c) is evidence that aggressiveness is the main cause of road accidents; (d) supports the view that driving conditions make drivers aggressive.

8 Taken at their face value, the figures for road accidents in the United States show that for both sexes the group with the highest mortality rate is (a) single; (b) married; (c) widowed; (d) divorced.

9 What hypothesis, not yet tested, has been advanced about the unsafe pedestrian?

10 What happens to drivers in middle age as their reactions become slower?

---

speed......... w.p.m. (page 241) comprehension..........(page 237)

Comments

Death Rates – Table 16. The point of the text is that the death rate increases in this order: married, single, widowed, divorced, in accordance with the 'way of life'. With this in mind, the columns of figures can be compared rapidly.

The evaluation of the evidence is very important in a study of this kind. 'It is possible that', 'It may be that', 'This tends to support the view', 'No evidence is yet available', and 'Caution in their interpretation' are parts of the text that cannot be ignored.

Exercise 8 (1380 words)

RESOURCES OF THE NILE*

by Michael Adams – *Guardian*, November 1963

---

starting time

WITHOUT the Nile Egypt is nothing. Apart from the scattered oases in the Western Desert and the coastal areas along the Mediterranean and Red Seas, the Nile Valley is the only habitable area of the country, and for centuries the river has provided Egypt's entire water supply, its chief means of internal communication, its only source of power, and the basic factor in its complex and vital pattern of agricultural development.

Until the nineteenth century this pattern had remained vir-

---

* Reproduced by permission of the editor of the *Guardian*.

tually unchanged since the days of the Pharaohs. The flood waters of the Nile, which reach Egypt in summer after the rainy season far to the south in the highlands of Ethiopia, were diverted by irrigation canals on to as much as possible of the land lying on either side of the river; when the flood subsided, the peasants gathered their single crop for the year, and lived on it until the yearly miracle was repeated. Occasionally Nature failed them and there was famine; sometimes the flood was excessive and washed away their mud villages and drowned their live stock. Either way the Egyptians accepted with resignation an apparently unchangeable and on the whole beneficent natural cycle.

During the nineteenth century the first attempts were made to control the Nile's flow and augment its benefits. A series of barrages were constructed which culminated in the great dam at Aswan (completed at the turn of the twentieth century), and these gave the Egyptians some freedom from the river's dictation. They made it possible for two and even three crops a year to be grown on the same land – and incidentally caused a boom in land values which caused the first faint disturbances in the pattern of land ownership.

AT the same time reforms in government and modest improvements in the standard of living of the peasants (especially in matters of health) caused a rapid expansion in the birth rate and a resulting population explosion. In the first 50 years of the twentieth century the population of Egypt doubled, while the country's resources remained practically unchanged, and the benefits of the improvements in irrigation and agricultural techniques were dwarfed by the number of new mouths that had to be fed. This was the situation that confronted the new rulers of Egypt after the revolution in 1952, which destroyed a corrupt monarchy and put in its place a group of young and completely inexperienced Army officers.

At first they thought that the country's basic problems could be solved by a reform of the social structure, which would destroy the hold of a few rich landowners on Egypt's immense agricultural resources and provide the incentive for peasant owners to co-operate in the production and marketing of their crops. Cotton, which had been introduced with great success in the nineteenth century, provided by 1952 some 80 per cent of Egypt's foreign exchange earnings, but the cotton trade was largely in the hands of foreigners and wealthy Egyptian entrepreneurs; if these could be controlled, or dispossessed, perhaps the economy could be made strong enough to face the demands that must be made on it.

This dream faded quickly. Even the scheme of land reforms which the young officers put into effect soon after their seizure of power (with a speed and efficiency which no succeeding revolutionary Government in the Middle East has been able to rival) only affected about 5 per cent of the total cultivated area and a little over 100,000 farmers; its value as an expression of the social policy of the new regime was considerable – but its importance from an economic point of view was negligible. What was needed, it was clear, was some radical change of policy, some altogether new departure in the whole approach to the problem of finding food and employment for a population which was increasing by almost half a million people every year.

THE obvious answer was industrialisation – obvious, that is, in economic theory, but immensely difficult to put into practice in the context of Egypt's resources, both of raw materials and of human traditions and aptitudes, and most difficult of all in view of Egypt's international situation. In 1952 there was still in effect a British Army of occupation in Egypt, and the first aim of the revolutionary Government – taking precedence even over its ambition to raise the standard of living of the Egyptian people – was that of making Egypt genuinely free and independent, putting an end to centuries of foreign domination and exploitation.

The struggle to achieve full independence set Egypt's economic advancement back by several years. The revolutionary Government's attention was absorbed by political questions, and it was not until the summer of 1956 that the last British troops were evacuated; no sooner had they gone than the

Egyptians, thinking now to turn to the execution of schemes which had been maturing for industrialisation and economic growth, found themselves involved in the Suez crisis – and the spark which touched off the crisis was precisely the most ambitious and far-reaching of all these schemes, the project of the Aswan High Dam.

Nearly three years have passed now since President Nasser laid the foundation stone of the High Dam, and there is no point in reopening the old controversy over its financing. What is often overlooked, now that the Russians are building the dam and the Egyptians are at the same time financing other huge development schemes with money and credits provided by the Western Governments, is that the Suez crisis and its aftermath gave the original and vital impetus to President Nasser's industrialisation programme.

Before 1956 the Egyptian Government and its technicians were toying with various projects which lacked co-ordination and for the financing of which there was no adequate provision. Economic development was a necessity if poverty and ignorance and disease were ever to be overcome, but to devise and especially to finance an adequate development plan was practically impossible precisely because the Egyptians were poor and ignorant and subject to most of the ills that plague mankind.

FOUR factors, all of them arising out of the Suez crisis, enabled the Egyptians to break out of this circle: first, they acquired the revenues of the Suez Canal, which now amount to more than £50 millions a year; secondly, they acquired, by the nationalisation and expropriation of foreign concerns, a stock of capital and installations on which to base their future expansion; thirdly, they gained the aid of the Soviet Union in the building of the High Dam; fourthly, they were driven, by the stringency of a virtual international blockade in 1956 and 1957, to think and work in serious terms for their economic future.

The outcome of this interplay of economic and political pressures is the present five-year plan, which requires investments of £E 1,700 millions, and aims at increasing the national income by 40 per cent. Of this enormous outlay (which is twice as great as the total national income at the time of the revolution in 1952), 35 per cent is to be devoted to the development of industry – and even this does not include the further sums which are earmarked for the construction of the Aswan High Dam.

An annual industrial fair in Cairo gives the visitor an idea of the progress already made in industrialisation. The cotton textile industry has been greatly expanded and now satisfies Egypt's own needs and provides a surplus for export. There are assembly plants for cars, trucks, railway carriages, radio and television sets, refrigerators, and stoves. The iron and steel plant at Helwan processes the ore mined in Upper Egypt. Oil production at over four million tons a year is rising steadily and should meet the internal demand within the next five years. Consumer goods of all kinds which were imported until 1956 are now produced locally, and if their quality is uneven this is not surprising in view of the haste with which the whole industrialisation programme has been and is being implemented. The problems remain acute, and until the rate of population increase is brought under control the amount of headway that the Egyptians can make against them is marginal; but the effort that is being made is unparalleled in modern Egyptian history, and stands comparison with anything that is going on in the underdeveloped world today.

---

finishing time

QUESTIONS

1 What was the culminating achievement of the Egyptians during the nineteenth century?

2 What nullified the benefits of improvements in irrigation and agricultural techniques in Egypt during the first fifty years of the twentieth century?

3 What were the economic consequences of the land reforms in Egypt after the revolution in 1952?

4 After the initial period of social reform, what did Egyptians come to realize was the only solution to their problems?

5 Mention *two* ways in which Egypt obtained financial resources for her new developments.

6 The Eygptian five-year plan aims at increasing the National Income by (a) 20%; (b) 40%; (c) 60%; (d) 80%.

7 The production of a vital commodity should meet the internal demand within the next five years (by 1968). What is it?

8 In Egypt, consumer goods of all kinds (a) cannot as yet be produced; (b) are now produced locally; (c) are beginning to be produced and are of excellent quality; (d) are produced only in the main towns.

9 What could jeopardize Egypt's future?

10 In the author's opinion, the Egyptian effort (a) is unparalleled in the world today; (b) bears comparison with that of any other under-developed country; (c) cannot be sustained without foreign investment; (d) has resulted in a much higher standard of living all round.

---

speed.........w.p.m. (page 242) comprehension.........(page 238)

Comments

This article should be read fast. The first two paragraphs, which set the pace, are based on what everyone knows about Egypt, and contain the kind of information that can be anticipated with ease. Themes which might have been anticipated, after previewing, are population, food, industrialization, and finance, because they apply to every under-developed country. Add President Nasser and the Suez Canal, and the anticipation is complete.

'FOUR factors' stands out vividly at the beginning of a paragraph; the information that follows needs to be thoroughly digested. The final assessment of the Egyptian effort, particularly the restatement of the crucial problem of population, cannot be skimmed over.

Very slow readers can make heavy weather of articles like this, and in the end retain no more, and usually understand far less, than readers who have concentrated on the main issues.

Suggestions for Practice

Find the average of your speeds for the last two passages, and the average of your comprehension scores. Take these as your standard.

1. *Below 250 w.p.m.*

If your comprehension is below 7, you are probably concentrating too much on the individual words and spending too much time on inessentials.

If your comprehension is 7 or over and your speed much the same as it was when you started, you may be spending more time than you need on unimportant details or subsidiary points, possibly for fear of missing something.

If your speed is below 250 w.p.m., whatever your comprehension, you should benefit from the following practice. Take a light novel and read it a good deal faster than you would normally; do not push your eyes over the page – which is useless – but gain speed by concentrating *only* on the story or theme and the main events and situations. Make a mental summary of each chapter and test your comprehension by reading in your normal way. (This, of course, is an exercise; how a novel should be read, even a very light novel, is a matter of individual taste.)

2. *Between 250 and 350 w.p.m.*

Choose several articles that are not too long and not too difficult. Bear in mind what we have said on page 49 for speeds between 250 and 350 w.p.m. Preview (spending more time on this if your comprehension is below 7); read for the main points; summarize; and check your comprehension.

3. *Over 350 w.p.m.*

Pay careful attention to what we have said on page 49 for speeds over 350 w.p.m. If your comprehension is below 7, keep to articles that are not too long and not too difficult. Allow rather more time for previewing; read for the main points; summarize; and check your comprehension.

If your comprehension is 7 or over, read some longer articles, trying to *maintain* your comprehension. Preview (allowing proportionately more time according to the length of the article); read for the main points; summarize; and check your comprehension.

CHAPTER 5

THE EYES

MUCH of the interest in better and faster reading has centred round experiments into the nature of eye movements, and much ingenuity has gone into devising ways of training the eyes to do the right things so that better reading would follow as a natural consequence. There is, however, abundant experimental evidence that good and bad eye movements are the result of good and bad reading and are not themselves the cause of reading habits.

Eye Movements

The eye does not move continuously along the line of print because the very movement would produce only a vague blur. The eye can only see when it is still, for when it moves it goes at a tremendous speed, which does not vary and cannot be controlled. This is contrary to experience, for you seem to be able to move your eye as quickly or as slowly as you please and the movement seems continuous. If you look about the room you will find you can only see distinctly when your eye is still; and this applies even when it is travelling very slowly: for then it makes a large number of rapid movements or jumps and you see in the pauses between the jumps. The way in which you regulate the speed of the eye over a given distance is by varying the number of pauses.

The same holds for reading. Your eye covers the print in a succession of jumps and you read in the pauses or 'fixations' between the jumps, making fewer fixations when you read fast and more when you read slowly.

Here is the way a slow reader might read a line of print, the movements of the eye being represented by arrows and the fixations by dots:

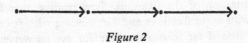

Figure 1

This might apply to a fast reader:

Figure 2

The Visual Span

Words are read on either side of each point of fixation in one unmoving glance or visual 'span'. The eye cuts the line of print into segments, taking snapshots like a camera; it does not read phrases, the mind does that. Nor does the eye fixate important words within the perceptual span. The manner of fixation is not understood, for sometimes the eye lands on the empty space between the words; all that can be said is that it seems to choose a point of vantage. The eye is like a movie camera, taking snapshots of the print; these the mind interprets as a continuous movement within the flow of meaning.

'Seeing' and Reading

Experiments have shown that when words are flashed on a screen for $\frac{1}{100}$ second the average reader, without any special training, can 'see' four related words totalling twenty-four letter spaces. If there were no more to it than this, he could read at 24,000 w.p.m., which still falls short of the 40,000 w.p.m. claimed for some prodigy in the United States. But when a span of words is read it has to be cleared by the brain, and this seems to take about $\frac{1}{5}$ second; and in reading, the spans have to be *related* for their meaning within a context. It is this that takes the time – *reading* as distinct from 'seeing'.

The most remarkable thing about reading is that the average duration of the fixations varies surprisingly little and for all practical purposes can be taken as approximately $\frac{1}{4}$ second for all adult readers, whether slow or fast; and this is only slightly more for difficult material, and only slightly less for easy material. The reason for this may lie in the time the brain needs to clear the information; whatever the cause, faster reading is not accompanied by any appreciable reduction in the average duration of the fixations. Slow reading, therefore, is equated with more fixations and fast reading with fewer fixations, because if we ignore the time for eye movements, the total reading time is the number of fixations at $\frac{1}{4}$ second per fixation.

Let us reconsider the two diagrams on page 79, but with the spans included.

Slow reader:

Figure 3

Fast reader:

Figure 4

The spans have been represented as flat ellipses. Actually the vertical extent of the span is one-half to two-thirds the horizontal distance, so that the reader can cover at least five lines of print with quite good reading vision. 'Vertical' vision plays an important part in reading and we shall refer to this when we consider skimming; but for our present purpose we can assume that the span is a flat ellipse.

The spans overlap a great deal, particularly in the case of the slow reader. But the slow reader cannot stop seeing and in fact sees the words several times over. The fast reader makes much fuller use of his spans and overlapping only occurs where it is most needed, in the less distinct parts of the spans, at either end towards the periphery. When the meaning is difficult, however, the fast reader also clusters his spans together, making more fixations and reducing his speed.

'Good' and 'Bad' Eye Movements

The photographic records of the eye movements of readers have been analysed and classified by specialists in this subject. We shall comment on the main points, refuting the categorical dos and don'ts they often inspire, which are based on a complete misinterpretation of the evidence. These are the characteristics of good readers:

1. Fewer fixations;
2. More rhythmical, in the sense of more regular, eye movements;
3. Fewer 'regressions' or backward fixations.

On the strength of this, the reader is often enjoined to make fewer fixations, move his eyes rhythmically, and refrain from regressing; and usually receives advice on how to widen his visual span.

The Case Against Training the Eyes

Fixations and Rhythmical Eye Movements

Informed opinion is that readers have no idea what movements their eyes are making and cannot control these movements with any degree of accuracy. We ourselves had the impression that when reading certain kinds of material we were making two fixations a line, but when we observed each other by means of mirrors we found we were making three or four fixations. If the reader tries to reduce his fixations consciously he can only do so by swinging his eyes in a regular rhythm, and not even the best eye movements have this degree of regularity. The essence of reading is flexibility; the reader has to vary his speed, often quite abruptly, according to the ease or difficulty of the material. The reader who starts swinging his eyes will swing them straight over the difficulties, where he should slow down. When we question readers on our courses, they assure us that they are never conscious of their eyes, never attempt to swing or push them, and only gain speed by trying to comprehend more efficiently.

Regressions

The experimental evidence is in line with the view that backward fixations are the result of difficulties in reading and do not cause them. Dr E. C. Poulton, of the Applied Psychology Research Unit of the Medical Research Council, has shown that if the reader is made to read through a small window that moves along the line of print his eye regresses even though the words can no longer be seen. It is useless telling the reader to stop regressing by 'trusting the eyes'; the remedy for constant regression is to concentrate on the meaning, not on the movements. Good readers glance back occasionally because a certain amount of regression is necessary for alert and constructive reading.

'Widening the Span'

The reader must certainly aim at understanding wider areas of meaning and so make better use of his visual span. The visual capacity of the average reader is astounding: as we have explained, he can 'see' an isolated span of three or four related words in $\frac{1}{100}$ second. Yet he scarcely manages to *read* a continuous text at the rate of two words in $\frac{1}{4}$ second. This does not mean, as some people seem to imagine, that the average reader should be able to read at least fifty times as fast; for the words must be cleared through the brain. What it does mean is that the reader only uses a fraction of his visual capacity.

Training methods often aim at 'widening the span' in the sense of *improving* visual capacity, the ability to perceive an isolated span of words; and this is borne out by the methods employed: flashing words on a screen, exposing words for a fraction of a second by some mechanical means, or making the reader run his eyes down the middle of a pyramid of words – so as to stretch his vision. But the problem is not how to 'see' an isolated span of words, for anyone can do this efficiently without training; but how to relate a succession of spans when they are *read*; how to understand the 'whole' meaning of a printed text. The evidence, supported by the recent research of G. Harry McLaughlin of the City University, is that exercises for widening the visual span have no effect on speed or comprehension.

We have placed the emphasis fairly and squarely on comprehension. Your eyes need no training; in fact, they cannot be trained to read better. But you cannot read without your eyes and the efficiency of reading is related to technical problems of seeing lines of print. We shall need to make further reference to the visual process in the following chapter on skimming.

A Note on 'Photographic' Memory

The mind is not a photographic plate; and the reader can no more take a mental photograph of a page of English than he can of a page of Chinese. Some readers, however, are able to *visualize* to a remarkable extent. But as we explained when dealing with vocalization and inner speech (pp. 62–4), what is important is not the nature and extent of the reader's imagery, but whether he learns by memorizing or by understanding.

If the reader who is a powerful visualizer tries to memorize the text, he has all the problems of the inefficient reader (for example, his images will have a way of reinforcing the trivial); and the further problem that visual imagery is notoriously inaccurate. If he reads for the meaning behind the words, he may imagine he has obtained a mental photograph of the page, but what he recalls is his own selective interpretation within the visual framework of the printed text. As long as the reader is not attempting to memorize the actual words, there is no reason why he should not have visual imagery to the top of his bent; he is a comprehending visualizer.

Many readers imagine that if only they had a 'photographic'

memory – in the literal sense of the word – their problems would be solved. This shows how easy it is to think of the mind as something completely passive and to forget that it is essentially selective and interpretative.

What to Do Next

Previewing

Allow 15 seconds for each of the next two passages. *Count this as part of your reading time.*

Reading

These passages contain examples and illustrations; so keep your reading flexible.

Comprehension

Both passages have ten multiple-choice questions.

Exercise 9 (1760 words)

SEEING AND BELIEVING*

by Professor J. Z. Young, B.B.C. Home Service, 1951

starting time

How often do we say 'Of course I believe it – I saw it with my own eyes!' But can we really be so sure what it is that our eyes tell us? For example, take the simple question, 'How big is the moon?' You remember the three jovial huntsmen in the nursery rhyme, how they hunted all night,

> And nothing could they find
> Except the moon a-gliding
> A-gliding with the wind.
> The first he said it was the moon.
> The second he said nay,
> The third it was a Cheddar cheese
> And half o' it cut away.

* Reproduced by permission of the author.

84

Could any of us make any better estimate of the moon's size if we had not read what astronomers tell us about its diameter? What does looking at the moon, or any other object, tell us about its real size? What do we mean by 'real' size, or 'real' shape, or other appearance, for that matter? Can we believe what we see of things; or rather, putting it the other way round, what do we mean when we say we believe that a thing has a certain size or shape?

Going back to the moon, you may say, 'Of course it is a long way off, and that's why it looks like a cheese.' But how do we know it is a long way off? Only because we cannot touch it or reach it by travel. Certainly this gives some help in finding out the significance, as we say, of its appearance. We interpret the image that falls upon the retina of our eye in terms of all sorts of other information we already possess, about distance and whether we can reach or touch an object. This shows at once that when we say that a thing appears to be of a certain size, we are not merely reacting to an image on the retina in the same way as we react to a simple stimulus such as a prick with a needle. When the needle pricks the skin, the nerves carry messages quickly to the spinal cord, and thence back to the muscles; the reaction is reflex. But when we look at something and speak about its size, the process involved in this reaction is much more complicated. The brain interprets the image on the retina in the light of all sorts of other 'information' it receives. Perception, in fact, is by no means a simple recording of the details of the world seen outside. It is a selection of those features with which we are familiar. What it amounts to is that we do not so much believe what we see as see what we believe. Seeing is an activity not only of our eyes but of the brain, which works as a sort of selecting machine. Out of all the images presented to it it chooses for recognition those that fit most nearly with the world learned by past experience.

It is very important for people like me, who study the brain, to try to form a picture of how such selection is done. How does this curious machine succeed in taking in so much information minute by minute, and fitting it together to produce useful actions that enable us to live our lives? Until we can answer such questions, our studies of how the brain works will remain incomplete. It is because we cannot easily imagine a machine that will perform such feats that we find it difficult to describe our behaviour as resulting from the actions of the brain. It is much easier to say that we act as we do because of some entity like the will, or super-ego, or something like that.

However, I do not want to pursue that theme now, but I want to give a few more examples to show how what the brain has learned influences the process we call 'seeing things'. Seeing, they say, is believing. But is it? An arrangement can be made such that a person looks through a peep-hole into a bare corridor, so bare that it gives no clues about distance. If you now show him a piece of white card in the corridor and ask how large it is, his reply will be influenced by any suggestion you make as to what the card may be. If you tell him that a particular piece is a visiting card, he will say that it is quite near. Show him the card at the same distance and tell him that it is a large envelope, and he will say that it is much further away. On the other hand, if you show a very large playing-card, say a Queen of Spades, he will say that it is very close, and if you show a tiny one he will say it is a long way away. Because, you see, playing-cards are nearly always of a standard size. In fact, the size we say things are depends upon what we otherwise know about them. When we see a motor-car from far away, its image on the retina is no bigger than that of a toy seen near, but we take the surroundings into consideration and give its proper size. We can get some clues about how we do this from the situations in which we judge wrongly. When we are in an aeroplane, the houses below us all look like dolls' houses. Why do we not see them at their 'proper' size, as we do distant houses in the country? Evidently we use the clues provided by the ground, with which we are familiar. We are not used to estimating the distance of objects seen far away with nothing in between.

For most situations, however, we have learned to interpret the images on the retina in the light of the framework in which they are set. When one comes into a room and looks around the walls, the pictures in their frames throw all sorts of curious shapes upon the retina. But we do not say that a particular picture frame is an irregular one with sides not parallel. We interpret the angles, and say that the frame is square or round, as the case may be. It can be shown that we do this largely by reference to the shape of the surrounding room. If the room is made to give false clues, we shall be misled in our reports about the pictures. This has been done in some experiments in America, in which people were made to look through a small hole into a specially made room with distorted walls. The sides of the room were not parallel and did not form right angles with each other, or with the ceiling. When perfectly ordinary pictures of people were hung on these funny walls, the viewers reported that the frames and faces had peculiar shapes, and they made all sorts of wrong statements about the sizes of objects in the room. But nobody said anything about the room being distorted. These recent experiments are only striking examples of visual illusions that have long been familiar. But we cannot dismiss them by the device of just labelling them 'visual illusions'. Why do we have these difficulties of interpretation? What can be learned about brain processes by studying such illusions?

Evidently one of the first rules of our seeing is that we must pick out a framework that is as familiar as possible. Presented with a situation in which we can say either that the room is crazy, or the pictures are distorted, we say the latter. The shape of the room is taken as our fixed frame of reference, and a crazy room is something not to be thought of. In fact, in seeing, we look for as much stability as we can get. If we saw everything photographically, the world would run past wildly every time we turned our heads, just as the pictures do when a movie camera sweeps around. But we learn to compensate for our own motion and for distance, and thus elect to see a much more constant picture than falls upon our eyes. Indeed, if we cannot pick out such a stable world, we become disorientated and terrified. Few things are more frightening than a uniform environment with no landmarks, whether it is an open sea, a mist, a forest or even a large dark room. This search for stability in perception is of course an aspect of the primal activity of all life – the search to remain intact in face of a hostile environment.

The naturalistic painter interprets his visual images in conjunction with the world of touch with which we are all familiar. He selects for attention the objects we can handle. This is indeed a sensible enough thing to do in a world where men work mostly with their bare hands and look with their unaided eyes. Perhaps the abstract painter paints differently because he has learned to live in a rather different world. Of course there have been abstractions in art since the cavemen began it. Is it true that modern abstractions are related to contemporary methods of thought? Nowadays we are surrounded by all sorts of mechanical and electrical tools. We read details of revelations by new instruments of strange aspects of things. You may reply at once that there is little evidence that abstract painters know anything of such matters. No doubt most of them would repudiate any interest in engineering or electrons. Nevertheless, they have moved in a world where there are many engines and their products, and where people constantly write and speak of such things. The whole intellectual climate of recent times encourages us to speak not only of things that we can touch, but of entities, such as atoms, that can only be revealed in elaborate ways, that is to say, are abstractions. It is not really far-fetched to suppose that the brain of the abstract painter shows by the designs it produces the effect of these ways of speaking. But it is very difficult to try to trace out in detail how our experience of the way in which the world can be made to meet our needs comes to condition what we see in it, and say or paint about it.

In a sense, therefore, our own world is the real one for each of us, and we can only interpret each new experience in terms of our own world. That is what I mean when I say that we see what we believe.

finishing time

QUESTIONS

1 Visual perception is concerned with (a) reflex actions, like all the other senses; (b) the simple recording of images; (c) the recognition of form, volume, and colour; (d) the selection of those features with which we are familiar.   ( )

2 Perception is an activity of (a) the eyes; (b) the eyes and the brain; (c) the eyes and the will or super-ego; (d) the eyes, brain, and something like the will or super-ego.   ( )

3 The idea that sums up the author's approach to perception is that (a) we do not so much believe what we see as see what we believe; (b) seeing is believing; (c) we must learn to remember what we see; (d) we cannot trust our eyes.   ( )

4 When we are in an aeroplane, houses look like dolls' houses because (a) the distance makes them look smaller; (b) we know they are a long way off; (c) we cannot really judge them in relation to their surroundings; (d) we are not used to estimating the distance of objects seen far away with nothing in between.   ( )

5 When people were made to look through a peephole into a specially constructed room with distorted walls hung with pictures of normal shape, they saw (a) distorted walls, but normal pictures; (b) normal walls, but distorted pictures; (c) distorted walls and distorted pictures; (d) normal walls and normal pictures.   ( )

6 The reason for the answer to question 5 is that (a) the distortion of the walls was so apparent it distorted everything else; (b) the pictures, being smaller, were stable visual units and remained unaffected by the distortion of the walls; (c) we do not expect to encounter distorted walls and so we do not see them distorted; (d) we see things photographically.   ( )

7 The author seems to imply that (a) the answer to problems of behaviour lies in the study of the brain; (b) mind and brain are related in ways we cannot fathom; (c) as the brain cannot do everything, we must postulate a will or super-ego; (d) when studying the brain, he believes what he sees; unlike the psychologists, who see what they believe.   (   )

8 Abstract paintings suggest that (a) the painter of today has reacted against mass production; (b) the painter believes in abstractions and therefore sees them and paints them; (c) the painter of today does not believe in what he sees; (d) the brain of the painter has been influenced by the abstractions of contemporary thought.   (   )

9 The author believes that in a sense our own world is (a) an unreal world; (b) the real world for each one of us; (c) a reflection of the real world; (d) the only world that is real.   (   )

10 If the author were asked to give his views on reading, he would probably say that (a) it would be an advantage to have 'a photographic memory'; (b) if the eyes were trained to see better, the reader would read better; (c) as the brain works like a curious machine, there is scope for mechanical methods of training; (d) we do not so much believe what we read as read what we believe.   (   )

---

speed.........w.p.m. (page 243) comprehension.........(page 235)

Comments

When the reader concentrates on the meaning and not on the actual wording, he becomes more sensitive to words *in their context* and to words that are constantly repeated because they are central to the author's theme. Make a list of the words (apart from 'seeing' and 'believing') that have struck you most in the last passage. Our own list is given at the end of the chapter, page 96.

Exercise 10   (1440 words)

ART AND ARTISTS

Extract from *The Story of Art** by E. H. Gombrich

starting time

There really is no such thing as Art. There are only artists. Once these were men who took coloured earth and roughed out the forms of a bison on the wall of a cave; today they buy their paints, and design posters for the Underground; they did many things in between. There is no harm in calling all these activities art as long as we keep in mind that such a word may mean very different things in different times and places, and as long as we realize that Art with a capital A has no existence. For Art with a capital A has come to be something of a bogey and a fetish. You may crush an artist by telling him that what he has just done may be quite good in its own way, only it is not 'Art'. And you may confound anyone enjoying a picture by declaring that what he liked in it was not the Art but something different.

Actually I do not think that there are any wrong reasons for liking a statue or a picture. Someone may like a landscape painting because it reminds him of home, or a portrait because it reminds him of a friend. There is nothing wrong with that. All of us, when we see a painting, are bound to be reminded of a hundred-and-one things which influence our likes and dislikes. As long as these memories help us to enjoy what we see, we need not worry. It is only when some irrelevant memory makes us prejudiced, when we instinctively turn away from a magnificent picture of an alpine scene because we dislike climbing, that we should search our mind for the reason of the aversion which spoils a pleasure we might otherwise have had. There *are* wrong reasons for disliking a work of art.

Most people like to see in pictures what they would also like to see in reality. This is quite a natural preference. We all like beauty in nature, and we are grateful to the artists who have

* Reproduced by permission of Phaidon Press.

preserved it in their works. Nor would these artists themselves have rebuffed us for our taste. When the great Flemish painter Rubens made a drawing of his little boy he was proud of his good looks. He wanted us, too, to admire the child. But this bias for the pretty and engaging subject is apt to become a stumbling block if it leads us to reject works which represent a less appealing subject. The great German painter Albrecht Dürer certainly drew his mother with as much devotion and love as Rubens felt for his chubby child. His truthful study of careworn old age may give us a shock which makes us turn away from it – and yet, if we fight against our first repugnance we may be richly rewarded, for Dürer's drawing in its tremendous sincerity is a great work. In fact we shall soon discover that the beauty of a picture does not really lie in the beauty of its subject-matter. I do not know whether the little ragamuffins whom the Spanish painter Murillo liked to paint were strictly beautiful or not, but, as he painted them, they certainly have great charm. On the other hand, most people would call the child in Pieter de Hooch's wonderful Dutch interior plain, but it is an attractive picture all the same.

The trouble about beauty is that tastes and standards of what is beautiful vary so much. . . .

What is true of beauty is also true of expression. In fact, it is often the expression of a figure in the painting which makes us like or loathe the work. Some people like an expression which they can easily understand, and which therefore moves them profoundly. When the Italian seventeenth-century painter Guido Reni painted the head of Christ on the cross, he intended, no doubt, that the beholder should find in this face all the agony and all the glory of the Passion. Many people throughout subsequent centuries have drawn strength and comfort from such a representation of the Saviour. The feeling it expresses is so strong and so clear that copies of this work can be found in simple chapels and far-away farmhouses where people know nothing about 'Art'. But even if this intense expression of feeling appeals to us we should not, for that reason, turn away from works whose expression is perhaps less easy to understand. . . . We may even prefer works of art whose expression is less obvious than Reni's. Just as some prefer people who use few words and gestures and leave something to be guessed, so some people are fond of paintings or sculptures which leave them something to guess and ponder about. In the more 'primitive' periods, when artists were not so skilled in representing human faces and human gestures as they are now, it is often all the more moving to see how they tried nevertheless to bring out the feeling they wanted to convey.

But here people are often brought up against another difficulty. They want to admire the artist's skill in representing the things they see. What they like best is paintings which look 'like real'. I do not deny for a moment that this is an important consideration. The patience and skill which go into the faithful rendering of the visible world are indeed to be admired. Great artists of the past have devoted much labour to works in which every tiny detail is carefully recorded. Dürer's water-colour study of a hare is one of the most famous examples of this loving patience. But who would say that Rembrandt's drawing of an elephant is necessarily less good because it shows fewer details? Indeed Rembrandt was such a wizard that he gave us the feel of the elephant's wrinkly skin with a few lines of his charcoal.

But it is not only sketchiness that offends people who like their pictures to look 'real'. They are even more repelled by works which they consider to be incorrectly drawn, particularly when they belong to a more modern period when the artist 'ought to have known better'. As a matter of fact, there is no mystery about these distortions of nature about which we hear so many complaints in discussions on modern art. Everyone who has ever seen a Disney film or a comic strip knows all about it. He knows that it is sometimes right to draw things otherwise than they look, to change and distort them in one way or another. Mickey Mouse does not look very much like a real mouse, yet people do not write indignant letters to the papers about the length of his tail. Those who enter Disney's enchanted world are not worried about Art with a capital A. They do not go to his shows armed with the same prejudices they like to take with them when going to an exhibition of

THE PROCESS OF READING

modern painting. But if a modern artist draws something in his own way, he is apt to be thought a bungler who can do no better. Now, whatever we may think of modern artists, we may safely credit them with enough knowledge to draw 'correctly'. If they do not do so their reasons may be very similar to those of Mr Disney. . . .

We are all inclined to accept conventional forms or colours as the only correct ones. Children sometimes think that stars must be star-shaped, though naturally they are not. The people who insist that in a picture the sky must be blue, and the grass green, are not very different from these children. They get very indignant if they see other colours in a picture, but if we try to forget all we have heard about green grass and blue skies, and look at the world as if we had just arrived from another planet on a voyage of discovery and were seeing it for the first time, we may find that things are apt to have the most surprising colours. Now painters sometimes feel as if they were on such a voyage of discovery. They want to see the world afresh, and to discard all the accepted notions and prejudices about flesh being pink and apples yellow or red. It is not easy to get rid of these preconceived ideas, but the artists who succeed best in doing so often produce the most exciting works. It is they who teach us to see new beauties in nature of whose existence we had never dreamt. If we follow them and learn from them, even a glance out of our own window may become a thrilling adventure.

finishing time

QUESTIONS

1 Art with a capital A (a) means the same thing in different times and places; (b) is art devoid of individual likes and dislikes; (c) does not really exist; (d) must be distinguished from commercial art.   (   )

2 According to the author, (a) there are no wrong reasons for liking a work of art; (b) we must not bring our memories to the enjoyment of a work of

art, but see it as it is; (c) there are no wrong reasons for disliking a work of art; (d) when responding to a work of art, we must rely on our instinctive feeling.   (   )

3   The beauty of the subject-matter of a picture (a) is often preserved by artists; (b) has no bearing on art; (c) is what inspires the artist's vision; (d) does not really determine the beauty of a picture.   (   )

4   Speaking of the beautiful, the author says that (a) tastes vary but standards do not; (b) tastes are determined by individuals, standards are determined by Art; (c) there are no standards, only tastes; (d) tastes and standards vary very much.   (   )

5   The author suggests that (a) it is often the expression of a figure in the painting which makes us like or loathe the work; (b) expression should never be obvious, but leave us something to guess and ponder about; (c) expression is the obvious, superficial aspect of art; (d) Beauty is changeless; it is only the expression of Beauty that changes.   (   )

6   Guido Reni's head of Christ is considered by the author to be (a) sentimental; (b) conventional and too easily understood; (c) an intense expression of feeling that is easy to understand; (d) a work that is overrated because of its subject-matter.   (   )

7   Paintings that look 'like real' (a) can be admirable works of art; (b) are not true art, because art has no concern with the real as such; (c) record every detail; (d) are best when they are produced with only a few lines.   (   )

8   Modern artists (a) are bunglers who can do no better; (b) draw things in their own way; (c) have a prejudice against drawing 'correctly'; (d) are so much concerned with their private visions that they ignore Art.   (   )

9   The distortions of nature that are often found in works of art (a) belong essentially to a more modern period; (b) are necessary in caricature; (c) are no

mystery and can be justified; (d) are not as appropriate when the subject-matter is beautiful in itself. (   )

10 In the author's opinion, the artists who often produce the most exciting works are those who (a) succeed best in discarding all the accepted notions and
prejudices; (b) are not afraid of being conventional;
(c) see things as children see them; (d) seem to belong to another planet.   (   )

---

speed.........w.p.m. (page 242) comprehension.........(page 235)

Comments

The author begins each paragraph with a clear proposition,
which he proceeds to support, or with the expression of a
popular view, which he then discusses. This orderly presentation makes the reader's task much easier.

Suggestions for Practice

Use your judgement, practising in any of the ways we have
suggested.

If you have not made much headway do not be perturbed;
some improvement in efficiency is what one would normally
expect at this stage. In the first two chapters of Part II we
provide passages which you will read in a prescribed way: they
are exercises in fast, flexible reading.

Key Words (*Exercise 9*):

INTERPRET, SELECT, ESTIMATE, STABLE, FAMILIAR, EX-
PERIENCE, INFLUENCE, FRAME (of reference).

PART II

*

THE STRATEGY OF
READING

INTRODUCTION

The Techniques of Perspective

THE technical problems of reading are part of a larger technical problem of communication between author and reader. As we have seen, the author is obliged to express the wholeness of his thought in a linear sequence of words; the reader has to recreate this wholeness from the printed line. To reconstruct the author's wholeness of thought the reader must get a perspective on the words.

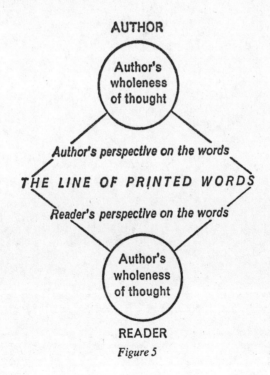

AUTHOR

Author's
wholeness
of thought

Author's perspective on the words

THE LINE OF PRINTED WORDS

Reader's perspective on the words

Author's
wholeness
of thought

READER

Figure 5

INTRODUCTION

Without perspective there can be no strategy of reading. The main purpose of Part II is the application of the techniques of perspective: SKIMMING (Chapter 6); ANTICIPATION (Chapter 7); ORGANIZATION (Chapter 8). Ideas are never neutral; so we have included (Chapter 9) ATTITUDES. The ability to retain and recall information depends on the way it is assimilated; MEMORY, which is the subject of Chapter 10, therefore serves as a general summary of reading as a digestive process. The application of these skills culminates in READING BOOKS, which is the subject of the concluding chapter.

CHAPTER 6

SKIMMING

A COMMON error is to identify good or bad reading, according to one's point of view, with skimming, which is a specialized skill of reading; the confusion arises because emphasis is laid on absolute speed rather than efficiency.

The applications of skimming are numerous and the ability to use the skill for a variety of purposes is the hall-mark of good reading: in everyday tasks it is strategy that counts, which could hardly exist without skimming. Nevertheless, it is just as important to be able to read very slowly as it is to skim; and as we shall see, skimming can be an aid to careful reading, and careful reading may prepare the way for skimming. Reading is a total process, of which skimming is but one highly important aspect.

We shall first consider the general method of skimming and follow this with the particular applications. The method and applications may seem a little complicated when explained, but skimming is not a difficult skill to acquire and great improvement can be made after only a few exercises.

1. The General Method

Skimming as a Process of Reading

Skimming is the technique par excellence *of perspective.* The reader who skims is like an observer on the look-out: he has a perspective; he keeps his eyes skinned; and he reacts with speed. Skimming is faster than fast reading, because the reader also uses the field of vision that lies outside his normal reading span. If a reader wanted to locate a number tucked away somewhere in the print, he would never waste time 'reading' till he found it: he would let it stand out in his total perspective of the page. If he wanted to find a particular word, he would try glancing down the page. Skimming is not some-

101

thing other than reading, but it is not fast reading in the accepted sense.

Skimming, though not fast reading, is nevertheless a process of reading. The reader who skims still has to relate what is given to what he already knows: words cannot leap unaided from the page into an empty, unprepared, and unexpectant mind. There is no magic in skimming. The observer, spotting planes, must have their characteristics clearly in mind. The reader who skims is an expectant observer, operating at great speed with small quantities of vital information. Skimming for specific information is fairly simple: the reader knows what he is looking for and can locate it by a process of *re*-cognition. It is like recognizing a face in a crowd. Skimming for general information is more complicated. If the reader 'knows nothing' about a difficult and completely unfamiliar subject and skims aimlessly over the pages, he will, of course, see many words and recognize what he chooses to recognize in the time available, but it will not be vital information and he will not be able to interpret it. If, on the other hand, he knows the subject from A to Z, the pages will seem to be alive with significant words corresponding to his own pattern of thought. But these are extreme cases. Usually the reader is helped by the unity of the text, which has a downward as well as a horizontal movement: one line, for example, may contain the subject; another, the verb; and another, the object or complement. Again, significant words that are constantly repeated, or words that reinforce one another, have a way of impressing themselves on the reader's attention. And the whole process is facilitated if the reader is able to anticipate the author's approach. In previewing, skimming may be combined with a brief sampling of the text: the sampling enables a pattern to form in the reader's mind: the clearer the pattern, the easier the skimming. In ordinary reading, the reader often obtains a sufficiently clear pattern of ideas to be able to skim with assurance over parts of the text.

Skimming is a vital part of ordinary reading. Skimming may occur whether the reading is fast or slow: it therefore increases the flexibility of reading and can produce speeds that cannot be measured by normal standards. Sometimes the meaning is so obvious that the reader only needs to read the first few words of a sentence: he can skim or even skip the rest. Sometimes he can go through paragraph after paragraph, keeping a general eye on the run of the words, so that he knows when to start 'reading' again. The art of highly flexible reading is to be able to let go of the words when this is appropriate, and to skim or skip without losing touch. Properly used, skimming does not introduce an element of superficiality into ordinary reading: by enabling the reader to eliminate unnecessary work and concentrate his effort where it is most needed, it increases the accuracy and sensitivity of comprehension.

We once tried a simple experiment. A group of readers, while being tested on a long passage containing a lot of unnecessary detail, received a signal every five seconds, and the moment they heard it, they automatically marked the place that they had reached. By comparing the number of words that were read during these five-second periods, we found that some of the fast readers had read certain significant parts of the text almost as slowly as the slow readers; but they had made up for it elsewhere and there was clear evidence of skimming. The readers with medium speeds were less flexible, though there was evidence of skimming. The slow readers seemed to take everything as it came, with little variation in speed, except that some of the irrelevant detail was read particularly slowly, instead of being skimmed. The fastest readers had the best comprehension.

Eye Movements

In skimming, the reader makes full use of the vertical extent of his vision. In Chapter 5 we mentioned that the normal reading span was between one-half and two-thirds the horizontal distance and covered at least five lines of print. Although in ordinary reading there is awareness of the lines above and below the one that is being read, the reader narrows his attention to a single line, and in Figures 3 and 4 we therefore represented his normal reading span as a flattened ellipse. Concentrate on a few words of print for a fraction of a second: you will have only the vaguest impression of what lies in the two or three lines above and below. Notice the difference when you open your attention to the five or six lines of print within your normal span. In skimming, the attention is kept open instead of being concentrated and the reader makes full use of his 'vertical' vision.

The rule still holds that the reader can only see when his eye is still. Very few fixations, however, are needed to cover the page with the quite good five-line vision of the normal reading span. Glance over a page of this book in three or four seconds: this is the kind of vision we mean.

The capacity to 'see' words is phenomenal. When the attention is open the words that are 'seen' exist as latent information. But in such a short space of time the reader is unable to comprehend this vast possibility of knowledge: the most he can do is to establish contact with a few of the words; which involves a process of selecting and relating. We have explained this process; all we need add here is that it can be assisted by the visual presentation of the material: headings, capitals, italics, paragraphs, and so on.

In skimming, there is no 'good' pattern of eye movements. It is interesting that readers who have heard nothing about eye movements often adopt ways of pushing their eyes over the page when skimming. Some zig-zag down the page, left, right, left, right. Others run their eye diagonally across their correspondence from top left to bottom right. Some run a finger straight down the middle of the page; others use two fingers. Some hop down the middle of the page, measuring the distance with their finger or with a pencil; others operate in the same way from the right-hand margin. It is fortunate that the eye does not respond slavishly to these directives, otherwise the methods of skimming we have mentioned would cause the reader to concentrate his attention quite narrowly at the points of fixation, which would make skimming virtually impossible.

Readers who have come under the influence of eye-movement theory, particularly the idea that regression should be avoided at any cost, are liable to suffer when skimming, because they imagine that the relatively free movement of attention, which is inevitable in skimming, is out of character with what they imagine should be a regular movement of their eyes.

The General Technique

The following is an account of what we ourselves seem to do – those points at least on which we can agree:

1. There is no conscious direction of the eyes.

2. The attention is open and takes in the whole width of the page: we find that words near the margins can easily mask one another.

3. There is a left–right movement to cover the horizontal extent of the page, though sometimes this is so quick that we seem to be going straight down the page.

4. Within this general movement our eyes, as far as we can judge, behave in a seemingly erratic manner, darting here and there as words attract our attention.

5. If a word strikes us forcibly, we explore the area round it.

6. The speed of skimming varies enormously: say from three to twenty seconds a page. There often seems to be a combination of fast reading and short skips. Sometimes there is what amounts to an erratic three-line reading.

7. When previewing, we combine skimming with sampling.

8. If the meaning is obvious, we skip and skim without hesitation or compunction, unless we are caught up in the author's mood or take pleasure in the words or the situation.

9. If we want to skip and be reasonably sure of our ground, we often read the first few words of each sentence.

10. Gradually, we have become more sensitive to less obvious expressions like 'The assumption is', 'In opposition to this', 'The outcome of this', announcing propositions or conclusions; which is a help both in ordinary reading and skimming.

2. Applications

Although we deal with these applications separately, we need hardly stress that in practice the reader may skim at one and the same time for a variety of purposes.

1. PREVIEWING

The essence of this is speed, for the aim is a quick impression. In general reading, between 10 and 20 seconds per 1000 words seems to be adequate for most purposes: sometimes a mere glance is sufficient; though in other cases previewing may be extended to cover the careful reading of key passages, like summaries and conclusions. Generally speaking, if the reader knows his subject well, he may only need to run his eye down the page. Normally the text has to be sampled. A common method of sampling is to read the first and last sentences of the first and last paragraphs, and the first lines of the other paragraphs, the assumption being that more meaning is to be found here than in places chosen at random, because a fair proportion of paragraphs begin with leading ideas and because the last sentences of the first and last paragraphs may contain conclusions. Do not adopt an inflexible procedure, however, as first and last sentences may be opening and closing formalities. If the author gives a clear indication of how the writing is organized, this may determine the course of the skimming.

Here are some examples of the many applications of previewing:

What to Read

Previewing can help the reader to decide whether it is necessary to read at all. In business, people complain that they get numerous documents marked 'for information', copies of anything their colleagues think they might conceivably be interested in, and slow readers may have no way of telling whether the effort is necessary, till they have finished reading.

When to Read

Previewing can also help the reader to plan his reading and establish an order of priority. This is particularly important if he has to ration his time: many things are left half read through no lack of intention. Planning by means of previewing is an aid to quick comprehension, for while the reader is tackling one assignment, he is unconsciously preparing the others. Previewing sometimes reveals that the reading can be postponed with advantage till the reader has had time to reflect on the subject.

How to Read

By previewing, the reader can determine his method of reading: whether the material can be disposed of with an extended preview; whether it should be read slowly, or quickly, or perhaps several times at different speeds. What is not generally realized is that two or more slow readings, particularly of long articles or books, are often no more rewarding than one, because they tend to follow the same pattern, and the main points are not necessarily emphasized when everything is repeated; a fast reading, followed by a slow one, is usually more effective. But without previewing, the reader has no way of deciding how to read.

2. SELECTIVE READING

The term 'selective reading' is used when the reader concentrates on selected aspects of the text. The art of selective reading is to locate the information by skimming; the reader should try to link the subject he has in mind with a closely associated pattern of words he can recognize in the text, telling him 'here' and 'not here'.

It is possible to narrow the search if the reader has an idea where the information is likely to be found within the general organization; and a preliminary skimming can sometimes show how the writing is organized.

3. ORGANIZATION

This is the subject of Chapter 8. We shall see that written material is sometimes organized in ways that can be easily discerned; if the organization conforms to a familiar type, then skimming should reveal this.

4. THE LOCATION OF SPECIFIC INFORMATION

The technique is much the same as for selective reading: skimming is easier if the information can be linked with closely associated words and if the general organization can be recognized. The operation, however, is not complete till the reader has made quite sure he has obtained the *right* information, by reading carefully.

5. IMMEDIATE REVISION

This is highly selective: hence the value of skimming. The reader may wish to memorize certain facts when he has finished reading, or return to a difficulty which has not been clarified by the general drift of the meaning. Revision can be much lighter work if the margins have been marked. A constructive method of general revision is to frame questions and to skim with these in mind.

6. LONG-TERM MEMORY

The use of skimming as an aid to retention is referred to in Chapter 10.

What to Do Next

In this book we are unable to provide the lengthy material we normally use for skimming practice; but by following our suggestions at the end of the chapter you can easily devise your own exercises. The most difficult part of skimming is using it to increase the flexibility of ordinary reading; we have therefore provided an exercise in which you will need to alternate constantly between skimming and careful reading.

The next passage compares 'universal histories' and what is called 'school history'. Your purpose is to read for information on:

1. The characteristics of school history.
2. The characteristics of universal histories.

Incidental detail is not required and you should skim over anything that is not essential information. Sometimes you may wish to skim at high speed or even skip; at other times to keep sufficiently in touch with the text to be aware of the implications. If you read flexibly you will have plenty of time for those parts of the text where the author make his points; you should not waste time on mere illustrations of his theme.

We do not suggest you would necessarily wish to read the passage in this way; it is an *exercise*.

PROCEDURE

1. Note your starting time.

2. Preview in the following way: sample the first and last *paragraphs* and the first *sentences* of the other paragraphs (if the first sentence is introductory, read further).

3. When you have finished previewing, do not pause, but start reading immediately. (*Your total reading time will include your time for previewing.*)

4. Summarize the essential points about (a) school history; and (b) universal histories.

5. Mark your summary by referring to the guide summary and marking scheme that follow immediately after the reading passage.

Exercise 11 (1950 words)

UNIVERSAL HISTORIES
from *The Bookmark* * by C. E. M. Joad

---

starting time

We all of us remember the kind of history we were taught at school. It was a queer sort of stuff, that aimed at doing two things; it endeavoured in the first place to nourish us on a diet of facts, and in the second to provide us with a set of correct opinions.

The facts consisted of isolated pieces of information. They told us the year in which William I. came to the throne, the Christian names of Edward III.'s wives, and what Henry VIII.

* Reproduced by permission of Miss M. F. Matthews.

had for his dinner on his fortieth birthday. In addition to the facts there were a number of legends. We were informed that one Clarence was drowned in a butt of Malmsey wine, and that George III. wondered how the apple got into the dumpling. The legends were more interesting than the facts, but were probably untrue.

Why we were told these things we did not know, and it is probable that our teachers knew no better than we did. Certainly we had no notion of what sort of people they were about whom these facts were recorded; we knew nothing of the lives they lived, the customs they observed, or the civilization they achieved. History, indeed, seemed to have little to do with people; it was full of kings and generals, of great men and of bad men, but of common men, who were neither great nor bad, it had nothing to say. To judge from the number of battles that figured in these records, the great men and the bad men, the kings and the generals, were a bloodthirsty lot, usually at each other's throats; but the extent to which the wars affected the civilian population was a matter on which history was silent.

Since the facts we had accumulated meant nothing to us, we forgot them as soon as we conveniently could, with the result that we grew up into men and women, and, what is more, into citizens governing a great Empire, and we knew nothing about history at all.

But our history teachers were not content that we should get our facts right; our opinions had to be right as well. Right opinions in this connexion means patriotic opinions. It is necessary that the young citizen should think his country deserving of support into whatever quarrel she may enter; her history, therefore, should be such as to win his admiration.

Since the histories of most countries are in the main disreputable, this result is achieved by a process of wholesale selection. Heroic episodes are magnified, discreditable ones omitted. We hear, for example, of how we won France under Henry V., but not of how we lost it under Henry VI.

The facts concerning the battle of Waterloo are well known, and there is a fair measure of agreement among historians as to the respective parts played by each of the three armies engaged. Nevertheless, the English child believes that Wellington beat the French unaided, the Prussians arriving only when the battle was practically decided; the German child that the English were within an ace of defeat from which they were saved only by the opportune intervention of Blücher; the French that Napoleon had practically won the battle, that in a certain sense he did win it, and that he was prevented from enjoying the fruits of victory only by a series of unforeseen coincidences so remarkable that no human being could have contended against them. These differing beliefs naturally result from the different selections from the facts upon which the children of the three nations are nurtured.

Within the last half-century, however, there has come into the world a new kind of history. It deals with peoples rather than with kings, it records movements and tendencies rather than births and battles, it tries to tell the truth rather than to manufacture opinion, and it is universal and not sectional.

By saying that it is universal I mean that it begins at the beginning – H. G. Wells's history starts some two thousand million years ago, when the earth, a red-hot nebula spinning in space, was first thrown off from the sun's mass, and ends with the Genoa Conference of 1922 – and it endeavours to recount the history of all countries instead of treating the world as a background to the history of one.

Now this universality in history is extremely valuable. It enables the reader to see the events of his own age, which taken by themselves appear to be of overwhelming importance, in their true perspective. Hitherto even the best historians had limited themselves to special periods or to particular countries. Grote had recorded the history of classical Greece, Mommsen of the Roman Republic, Gibbon of the decay of the Roman Empire. Within its limits each of these histories is a masterpiece, yet with regard to everything that falls outside them it is silent.

The best modern histories confine themselves to going over minute pieces of historical territory with a microscope, on the assumption that it is better to know one or two things accurately than to have a superficial knowledge of many. This assumption is clearly untrue. It is essential to get a bird's-eye view of the whole territory, before settling down to study any part in detail, and historians who concentrate on one tract and ignore the rest are like men who would draw up an Ordnance Survey map of an English county, but forget to mention that it is a county of England.

But how is a universal history possible? Can so much be brought within the confines of a single book? Only if the writer selects, and what he selects will depend upon what he thinks important. What he thinks important will depend again upon his likes and dislikes, his preferences and his prejudices. Hence any history which is not a mere record of facts will be an intensely personal and individual affair, reflecting the mind of the writer at the same time as it records the passage of events. Winwood Reade's *The Martyrdom of Man* is a case in point. He was struck by the fact that Africa was commonly supposed to be a continent apart, lying right outside the main stream of the world's affairs, and he wished, therefore, to write a history of Africa showing how profoundly Africa had affected the world, first through the influence of its religions, secondly through the growth of the slave trade. But in order to demonstrate the extent of Africa's influence on the world Reade found himself led insensibly into describing the world as well as Africa.

Moreover, he had read Darwin's *Origin of Species*, and was an ardent convert to the theory of evolution. He wanted to unfold the great chronicle of life, from those first living specks which floated about on the scum of the intertidal shores to the scientific achievements of the nineteenth century. His enthusiasm for evolution led him into violent hostility to revealed religion. Man, he held, was not a degenerate angel, but a promoted ape, and those who believed in a personal God, a Fall, a Heaven and a Hell were falsifying the teaching of evolution. In his history, then, Reade tries to describe the origin of religion as an outcome of fear, and to exhibit it as a phase through which man passes during the period of his adolescence, but with which he will be able to dispense when full grown.

What Reade calls, therefore, 'this long and gloomy period of the human race,' by which he means the religious period, will come to an end as soon as men achieve liberty and learn to regulate their lives by reason.

Reade's anti-religious sentiments caused his book to be universally execrated by the pious reviewers of the nineteenth century. Nevertheless, it sold like hot cakes. It was an entirely new thing in histories. Not only did it regard the whole of history from an African angle, in itself an unprecedented thing, but it really did begin at the beginning and end at the end. An additional attraction was Reade's wonderful style. He is witty, eloquent, extraordinarily clear, and never dull.

At any moment you may come across a passage such as: 'Animal heat is solar heat; a blush is a stray sunbeam; Life is bottled sunshine, and Death the silent-footed butler who draws out the cork'. And his account of the slave trade and of the agitation for its abolition is one of the most moving things in history....

The greatest of universal historians is H. G. Wells. Everybody has heard of *The Outline of History*. I am not going to pretend to review the *Outline*. I know that each expert on a special period, jealous, perhaps, of a man who insists on using his eyes instead of peering through a microscope, says that Wells is inadequate and misleading on his period, though he is no doubt very good on other people's periods, and I know that despite the experts the *Outline* is a very good book.

There are, however, just two points upon which I wish to touch, as showing the value of universal histories in general and of Wells's history in particular.

The first is, that a universal history must of necessity be a history of movements rather than individuals. Thus we get rid of the taint of kings and generals from the very beginning. Wells, for example, has a vivid chapter describing the Mongol invasions which in the thirteenth century established an empire that stretched right across Asia from China to the Black Sea. Perhaps because he is something of a nomad himself, Wells is extraordinarily good and vivid on the periodic incursions of nomadic outsiders, and the attention which he bestows upon them is one of the distinguishing features of his history. But whereas others have dramatized the Mongol leaders, Jenghis Khan and Tamurlane, Wells is concerned to describe the habits of the people, the effect of their impact upon the older civilization, and its reaction upon the Mongols themselves.

In the second place, Wells gives us for the first time a proper historical perspective. We get things 'oriented', as it were, and the effect of this orientation is to make us realize the novelty of civilization. It is an episode, one among many, the latest in the career of man, just as man is the latest episode in the career of the earth. 'It is barely a matter of seventy generations between ourselves and Alexander', 'half the duration of human civilization, and the keys to all its chief institutions are to be found before Sargon I.' (2570 B.C.); yet man is thousands of years older than the earliest institution, and for millions of years before man there was life.

It is this newness of civilization that in Wells's view affords the chief hope for the future. The facts of evolution are undoubted; life began as an eddy in the primeval slime: it culminates to-day in the brain of Mr. Wells. But some, while admitting the process, have doubted the progress. Mr. Wells, however, has no doubts. Evolution for him is progress, and when we point to the wickedness of man, his selfishness, his political childishness, his inability to behave himself or to keep his hands off his neighbours, Wells has simply to emphasize his youth. Civilization is in its childhood, and we are mere babies, with the instincts of babies, to whom, however, science has opened a vista of infinite possibilities.

History, in short, for Wells reveals to us 'a being at first scattered and blind and utterly confused, feeling its way slowly to the security and salvation of an ordered and coherent purpose'.

---

finishing time

---

speed.........w.p.m. (page 243) comprehension.........(page 115)

UNIVERSAL HISTORIES

School History

    Isolated facts.

    Legends.

    Correct opinions (patriotic).

    Process of wholesale selection.

Universal Histories

    Movements, peoples, trends.

    Historical perspective: all countries, all time.

    Selective and therefore intensely personal, and to some extent biased.

    But an evolution towards coherence and truth; no wholesale selection (as in school history).

MARKING

Use this summary as a guide and do not interpret it literally. We suggest the following marking scheme:

School History – 4 marks (1 for each point).

Universal Histories – 6 marks ($1\frac{1}{2}$ for each point).

Your assessment may differ from ours: you may wish to group or separate the points, add points, or alter the allocation of marks. Use your judgement. As good a method of marking as any is a general impression with the main points in mind; rigid adherence to a marking scheme can often go seriously awry.

Comments

The meat of the article comprises only a small part of the text; by skipping or skimming the illustrations we can obtain a clear understanding of the author's theme – which was the purpose of the exercise.

When previewing, we see at a glance in the first paragraph: 'in the first place' – *facts*; 'in the second' – *correct opinions*.

115

The last paragraph has 'in short' – Wells (i.e., universal histories) – *ordered and coherent*. Freely skimming over the first sentences of the other paragraphs, we are arrested by: 'just two points ... value of universal histories ... the first is' – *movements rather than individuals*; 'in the second place' – *historical perspective*. (Even if we had not been told, we would have noticed that there were many illustrations.) The information we have gained is more than enough to set us thinking or, at any rate, to set in motion the unconscious work of preparation and anticipation that enables us to use our knowledge and read actively.

Most readers who do this exercise try to assimilate too much information for the *given purpose*. Some go into detail over the Battle of Waterloo, which in itself is not important – the Spanish Armada would have served just as well, while others make references to Wells, Darwin, and Reade. Those who give unnecessary detail have often read this passage too fast for *their* purpose and, it seems, at a fairly uniform speed, because the vital points about the methods of selection – *School History* and *Universal Histories* – are often missed; and there may be surprising misinterpretations to the effect that universal histories are anti-religious or characterized by personal likes and dislikes, prejudices and preferences – usually verbatim. In general, readers do not pay enough attention to the final 'in short' paragraph and miss the significance of the key expression 'selection'.

Exercises like this can give rise to misunderstanding. Readers sometimes say that they do not read this kind of material in their work. We can only reply that they may have to read documents containing ancillary information of interest to some, but not to them; or perhaps material interspersed with statistics or technicalities that can be studied to greater advantage once the general framework has been understood. It is the *technique* that counts; and in our opinion it is better for readers to practise on material they do not read habitually. Again, it is never our intention to advocate that illustrations should always be skimmed, for it may not be possible to grasp the meaning till they have been understood, and in any case they may be of absorbing interest: it is a question of purpose, the reader's knowledge, and the nature of the material; in 'Universal Histories' it was *possible* to skim the illustrations, and this enabled us to contrive an *exercise* in flexible reading.

Suggestions for Practice

1. Read a few words of the first sentence of an article; then open the attention so as to locate the beginning of the next sentence and read the first few words of that. Repeat this down the page. The purpose of this exercise is not to understand the meaning, but to practise the free movement of attention within an enlarged area of vision.

2. Read one of the previous reading passages several times till you are quite familiar with the contents. Repeat the exercise given above, but reading sufficient of each sentence to grasp the trend of the meaning. The purpose here is to practise releasing one's hold on the print once the meaning of a sentence has been understood – anticipated – from the first few words. (You are practising a skill; this is not a rule of reading.)

3. Get someone who has just read an article to ask you to find one of its main ideas. This is a good exercise because it requires a battery of techniques: skimming for the general organization, sampling the text, selective reading ('possibly here', 'definitely not there', with a pattern of words in mind), skipping, and skimming freely. Do not, however, become preoccupied with methods as such; after a few exercises you should become adept at finding your way through the maze of words with *method*; it is surprising how quickly readers acquire the knack.

The object of the exercise is to locate the idea, not to understand the text, though you will, of course, pick up a lot of information by the way, more perhaps than you thought possible. The value of the exercise is that one learns how to sense the *kind* of meaning that is in the text, without going through the entire process of assimilation; this is a major skill, as frequently one does not wish to pursue a point that is obvious, familiar, complicated, technical, or not germane to one's purpose; it is a question of when to hold fast to the text and when to relax or release one's hold.

4. *The Extended Preview.* Take an article of between 1000 and 2000 words and preview for approximately 1 minute per 1000 words; then read it through as flexibly as you can for a general understanding. Make a summary and test your comprehension. You may find it interesting with this technique to know your speed.

If you are a slow reader, the knowledge gained by previewing will impel you forward when you come to read.

CHAPTER 7
ANTICIPATION

Using One's Existing Knowledge

WE shall consider anticipation as an aspect of the process of reading: how the reader anticipates while he is reading and how he is able to anticipate even before starting to read; in other words, how he makes use of his existing knowledge.

1. Anticipating While Reading

Anticipation means that the reader's mind is ahead of his reading, preparing the way. This forward projection of the mind is characteristic of all mental activity. Consider an interview. As it proceeds, the interviewee may be able to sense the trend of the questions and make reliable predictions, on the strength of which he prepares his answers in advance. The reader is in much the same position: as he warms to the topic he becomes actively engaged in predictive thinking, which enables him to prepare the ground and apply his own knowledge.

Predictive Thinking

Small ideas lead to small predictions, and the reader who comprehends too narrowly restricts his anticipation and makes inadequate use of his existing knowledge. In Figure 6 the reader has obtained a small-sized idea (A), and his anticipation is restricted (B).

Little predictive thinking

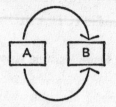

Limited use of the reader's existing knowledge

Figure 6. Poor Anticipation

In Figure 7 the reader has grasped a sizeable idea (A), and consequently has been able to anticipate constructively (B) and make full use of his knowledge.

Good predictive thinking

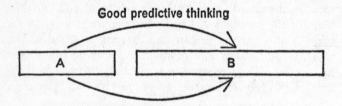

Full use of the reader's existing knowledge

Figure 7. Good Anticipation

Suppose the reader obtains only fragmentary impressions (A[1], etc., in Figure 8):

Retrospective comprehension

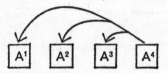

Figure 8. No Anticipation

He may fail to grasp the meaning till he has reached A^4, so that he has to retain A^1, A^2, and A^3 and comprehend retrospectively. Retrospective comprehension is, of course, a necessary part of reading; but if the reader is constantly preoccupied with needless arrears of comprehension, he cannot possibly think ahead and use his knowledge; he cannot anticipate.

There is a minimal amount of anticipation in even the slowest reading, otherwise the reader would have to keep pausing to decide between the many different uses of words, as primitive peoples do when they learn English: their culture is lacking in certain basic ideas and modes of thought, which makes it difficult for them to anticipate the meaning of certain English words. We all gain speed from the structure of the language, and from a multitude of familiar phrases that can be anticipated in a flash from the smallest cue; but even this bonus of speed can be wasted by poor reading.

2. Anticipating Before Reading

The reader is able to anticipate before actually starting to read, because of his knowledge. Obviously, the more knowledge he has of a topic, the easier it is for him to anticipate it; but we are thinking primarily of general approaches. Here are some examples of what we mean. 'Business Forecasting' – we might think of a related topic, forecasting the weather, and begin: 'Time – short-term, long-term. Space – local, regional, national.' Then we could ask a few questions: 'Accuracy? Method? Speed? Cost? Purpose?' Articles such as 'Housing', 'The Employment of Graduates', 'Women in Industry', 'The Shortage of Teachers', 'Power Cuts', might well have the same structure – demand and supply, about which everyone is knowledgeable without the slightest knowledge of economics as a subject; it is part of our common culture. General reading is for general consumption; and without any kind of specialized knowledge the reader can often approach the most unlikely subjects: 'Combine Harvesters', for example, a topic suggested by a reader as one that could only be anticipated by a specialist. This is what came quite spontaneously from a reader in a group, who had no recollection of ever having read an article on the subject: 'Where used? United States. Large farms. Small British farms – hedges. Large capital outlay. Co-operative ownership? Government subsidies? Need for technicians on farms. World food problem. Under-developed countries? Uses for famine relief?' And when the group joined in, there was a rush of ideas and questions. It is surprising how accurate these anticipated approaches can be; but far more important than accuracy is the process of preparation: inaccurate predictions before reading can lead to good anticipation while reading, because the reader is expectant and responsive. The key to anticipating the author's approach is questioning: this *opens* the mind and releases a spontaneous flow of ideas and further questions; concentrated thinking without questioning does not open the mind so effectively.

The value of anticipation is that the reader can warm to the topic: once reading begins, the reader is obliged to concentrate his attention; and if he starts cold may easily acquire a mental 'set', a predisposition to think along rigid lines, the lines of print, in fact; he is much less likely to read responsively and use his own knowledge and far more likely to allow his thinking to be done for him by the author.

It is for this reason that we recommend the exercise of anticipating the topic before starting to read. Frequently, there is no conscious anticipation before reading, because the article is short and the topic easy and familiar. Preliminary anticipation is usually combined with previewing, so that the reader has something to go on. Sometimes there is lengthy anticipation without previewing: we can think of two directors who spent half an hour discussing a document before attempting to read it, deciding what they wanted to find in it and what they feared might be omitted. In the reading of lengthy articles and books, anticipation and previewing are indispensable skills.

What to Do Next

The next passage is an exercise in pure anticipation, so there will be no previewing. As we shall anticipate the structure of the article, this will also serve as an introduction to the next chapter on 'Organization', where we shall consider some of the more familiar ways in which writing is organized. In the present exercise there will be scope for spells of fast reading verging on skimming; we shall prescribe the method so as to make the practice as effective as possible.

PROCEDURE

Here is the title:

'What happens when you expose a group of young business executives to Joyce's *Ulysses* and the *Bhagavad Gita?* ...

BELL TELEPHONE'S EXPERIMENT IN EDUCATION'

From this we gather that it is a popular account of a social *experiment*. An experiment of this kind *must* take the form:

PROBLEM – EXPERIMENT – RESULTS – CONCLUSIONS.

You are therefore required to read for answers to the following questions.

1. WHAT WAS THE PROBLEM OF THE FIRM?
(Why did the firm think it necessary to send men on such a course?)

2. WHAT WAS THE NATURE OF THE EXPERIMENT?
3. HOW DID THE MEN REACT TO THE EXPERIMENT?
4. WAS THE EXPERIMENT SUCCESSFUL?
(How did the men behave when they returned to their jobs? Was the firm satisfied?)

Study these questions; modify them if you wish, or expand them along the lines we have indicated. Then read the passage *only for answers to questions.* You cannot skim this article as freely as you could 'Universal Histories'. Where there is much detail, be on the alert for the implications and, if necessary, obtain a representative sample of the facts. In any popular exposition there are certain to be incidental passages with a strong human appeal; these, *for the purpose of the exercise,* you can skim, using your questions like a magnet to draw out anything that is pertinent.

Write a summary: 250 words should be ample. Mark this by referring to the guide summary and marking scheme that follow immediately after the reading passage.

Exercise 12 (3390 words)

What happens when you expose a group of young business executives to Joyce's *Ulysses* and the *Bhagavad Gita*? . . .

BELL TELEPHONE'S EXPERIMENT IN EDUCATION *
by E. Digby Baltzell. *Harper's Magazine*, March 1955

starting time

On June 23, 1954, thirty-one children and their parents were enjoying themselves at a picnic on the lawn in front of an old colonial farmhouse in Media, Pennsylvania, a suburb of Philadelphia. Many of the children were a long way from home: Melinda and Gayleen Woodruff lived in Palo Alto, California; Sally, Sue, and Cindy Hoverstock came from Houston, Texas; and Judy and Dick Ansel had just driven up from Little Rock, Arkansas. They would all be driving home across America the next day. These children had come to visit their fathers, a carefully chosen group of businessmen from the Bell Telephone System, who were celebrating their completion of a novel experiment at the University of Pennsylvania. These young executives were, perhaps more than they knew, pioneers.

Many leaders in American business have been frankly worried about the supply of broadly educated executives for top management positions. Talented and conscientious young men who are now climbing the large-corporation ladders too often exhibit the 'trained incapacity' of the narrow expert, and for understandable reasons: many of them are recruited from business and engineering schools rather than liberal-arts colleges. Moreover, the pressure of their jobs narrows rather than expands their interests in the world about them.

The Bell system, with more than 700,000 employees, is the biggest industrial organization in America. To keep its tremendous daily traffic of calls, installations, and services humming requires, of course, a vast army of technically trained specialists. But there is nothing static about this business and at the policy level executives are continually forced to solve new problems and find fresh answers to old ones. For some time the Bell system's top management has been worried about over-specialization among its younger executives, the very men who are ultimately going to have to be the system's imagination.

W. D. Gillen, President of the Bell Telephone Company of Pennsylvania and a trustee of the University of Pennsylvania, determined several years ago to find some way of broadening the educational background and expanding the point of view of Bell's most promising young men. In 1952 he discussed with the representatives of the University of Pennsylvania a new kind of education for executive leadership – together they decided that in contrast to the usual executive *training* program, young executives needed a really firm grounding in the humanities or liberal arts. A well-trained man knows *how* to answer questions, they reasoned; an educated man knows *what* questions are worth asking. At the policy level, Bell wants more of the latter.

Mr. Gillen took the plan to several other presidents of Bell companies and got their support. In the spring of 1953, as a consequence, the Institute of Humanistic Studies for Executives, sponsored by Pennsylvania Bell, came into existence on the campus of the University. Classrooms and administrative space were assigned, and Dr. Morse Peckham, an associate professor of English who had outlined a liberal-arts course for businessmen the previous autumn, took on the job of director.

The first group of Bell executives arrived the following September and, as a member of the faculty assigned to keep close tabs on the experiment, I got to know them and their problems well. There were seventeen of them, a carefully chosen lot from various sections of the country. But they were all from the middle levels of management. Eleven were between thirty-five and forty years of age, three were in their early thirties, and one was forty-eight; their average length of service with the Bell system was thirteen years; all were married and all, save one, were fathers; fifteen were college graduates, nine had B.S. degrees, and six had B.A.s.

Each of them was granted a ten-months' leave of absence with full salary from his regular job in order to devote his full time to the Institute. The first nine months of the program included 500 hours of lectures, discussions, and seminars. The final four weeks of the program were set aside for a reading period during which the men were entirely on their own.

To jar the businessmen-students out of the job atmosphere from which they had come, the courses were deliberately arranged so as to proceed from unfamiliar ideas and material to those closer to their own lives and experience. In the early months of the program the men received a highly concentrated dose of systematic logic, the study of Oriental history and art, and the reading of such works as the *Bhagavad Gita*, *Monkey*, and the *Tale of Genji* – a far cry from the American suburban groove and business routine. By December many of the students were depressed – the 'Bagdad Geisha,' they felt, was a waste of time.

On the other hand, as the end of the program approached, the men were prepared to bring a wide-ranging intellectual experience to bear on problems much closer to home. In the final and most popular course, American Civilization, they spent twelve weeks discussing such problems as: the making of the Constitution; the Haymarket Riot and the industrialization of America; *Sister Carrie* and the revolution in American sex mores; *Main Street* and the disillusionment of the 1920s; and *The Lonely Crowd* and American character structure. The course was organized on the theory that one approaches Carol Kennicott's struggles with Main Street from a broader point of view for having known something about Prince Genji in tenth-century Japan.

Through James Joyce's Ulysses

The study of James Joyce's *Ulysses* was the most controversial part of the curriculum. It was the director's pet idea, and he fought for it. To him it symbolized the function of a liberal-arts education – to provide a liberating experience and to stimulate the intellect. He believed that an intensive analysis of Bloom's day in Dublin, June 16, 1904, would do just that. (One of the students sent postcards to the other participants on June 15, 1954. On the card was written: 'Happy Bloom's Day.')

The *Ulysses* course consisted of eight three-hour seminars for each of two groups of students. Fortified with the extensive 'pony' literature on Joyce, dictionaries of mythology, encyclopedias and Webster, each man prepared one or more reports for his seminar group.

They found it a challenging, and often exasperating, experience. At the close of each report, there was a sigh of relief from the man who had to report, and a wave of congratulations from the rest of the students: 'I was proud of Gene! I never got half the stuff he saw in the chapter when I read it.' And neither had anyone else, on even a careful first reading.

The final report in one of the *Ulysses* seminars suggests the tone of the whole program. The man who gave it was an accountant and, incidentally, a musician who had earned his way through college during the Depression by playing in dance bands. Patently cool toward the works of Mr. Joyce, he finally volunteered to report on Chapter XI, the 'Sirens' section, in which Bloom's extreme loneliness is portrayed in a highly complicated and technical musical theme. His report took just forty-two hours to prepare. 'You know, this man Joyce has something for everybody if he looks hard enough. I really got interested in that — chapter.' The report was so thorough that the instructor had it mimeographed for distribution to the whole seminar group and for the use of his future graduate students.

The Institute courses were taught by several members of the faculty from the University, supplemented by two professors from Bryn Mawr and Swarthmore colleges. In addition, to make sure the students came in contact with the best in the intellectual world, each instructor was asked to invite a series of guest lecturers. One hundred and sixty of America's leading intellectuals – including Lewis Mumford, Clyde Kluckhohn, W. H. Auden, Jacques Lipchitz, Delmore Schwartz, Henry S. Commager, Virgil Thomson, Ludwig Lewisohn, David Riesman, and Eric Goldman – visited West Philephia last winter.

The guest lecturers were interested both in the nature of the experiment and in the men who were participating in it. In a club room rented in a hotel near the University they had a chance to meet the students at the cocktail hour for informal discussion. 'You mean,' one of them said to me, 'that this idea came from the Bell Telephone people!' Public relations cut both ways in these meetings. The distinguished visitors became acquainted with and, above all, were appreciated by the students.

For ten months the seventeen Bell men were kept busy. In addition to the regular classwork, they read constantly (more than the average graduate student); they went on formally planned trips to art galleries, museums, and historical sights in Washington, New York, and Philadelphia; a block of seats was reserved for them at the Philadelphia orchestra; and they visited and studied in some of the distinguished examples of residential and institutional architecture in the city.

All of the men seemed determined to make the most of the experience. Not only did they want to justify the costs of the program to the Bell system, but they seemed to want to make up for what they had missed in their formal education. 'College wasn't like this, or at least I never found it so,' some of them said, and one graduate engineer told me: 'It was the degree as a ticket to a job, not an education, that we were after in those Depression days.'

Aspirin After Poetry

In Utopia, perhaps, men will be 'trained' in their teens and 'educated' in their thirties. While twenty may be the best age for learning mathematics, chemistry, or engineering, maybe *Hamlet* or *Faust* are better understood in maturity. To these students, a discussion of pragmatism was naturally related to their own anxieties about permissive education (one father, trained in a teachers' college, disciplined his child without feeling guilty about it for the first time during this period); *Babbitt* or C. Wright Mills' *White Collar* suggested disturbing insights into their own lives; and these men who had lived through the Depression knew what Walt Whitman was giving up when he left a well-paying editorship to devote his life to poetry, even if they could not quite understand his motives.

A real education is an emotional as well as an intellectual experience; and there were both pleasant and unpleasant experiences in this first year's experiment. Few of the students, for example, will ever forget the lecture on Leonardo Da Vinci in the art class or the reading of Ezra Pound's *Pisan Cantos*.

One morning in May a student described the slide-illustrated lecture on Leonardo to me over a cup of coffee at Horn and Hardart's restaurant. When the class was over, so his story went, the lights were turned on and the instructor walked out of the room with tears in his eyes; after several minutes of silence, the students filed out behind him. The eyes of this tall Lincolnesque executive, a Lieutenant-Commander, USNR, who had seen the bomb damage at Nagasaki, were somewhat moist that morning as he described the lecture on Leonardo.

The poetry of Ezra Pound is still a controversial artistic fact. Whereas many young graduate students follow fashion, and either like Pound or not as the intellectual climate demands, his *Pisan Cantos* were an unpleasant emotional issue at the Institute. On a Wednesday evening in February, during a heated and somewhat tense discussion of Mr. Pound's poetry with a visiting expert from Harvard, there was very little sympathy for either the guest's admiration for the *Pisan Cantos* or his friendship for Mr. Pound. Driving home after the discussion, one of the students said: 'You know I was so upset reading Pound last Monday night that I took two aspirins before going to bed and then got up at two in the morning to take a sedative before finally getting off to sleep. I could not, for the life of me, understand what the man was trying to say in those *Cantos*.'

'This is my one big opportunity,' one of the men said to me after he had been in the course for several months, 'and I mean to make the most of it.' This sense of cramming into a short ten months what might have been for many several years of education raised several questions. Were these men interested primarily in doing a good job in the Institute because it might mean later promotions in the Bell system for them? Having been exposed to an experience that would presumably change their attitudes towards their jobs and their leisure, was there a chance that they would never again be satisfied with the struggle up the corporate ladder? These were questions that those of us on the faculty asked ourselves, and some of the answers became apparent during the course of the year. Others will remain unanswered for some time.

The Lasting Effects

The Institute of Humanistic Studies for Executives, we were confident, introduced seventeen men of affairs to a new world of ideas, new values, new interests, and to a new type of personality, the intellectual; and the men of affairs changed considerably. They have taken to buying books and building their own libraries; they are collecting classical records; they think about replacing 'wall-cover' with art in their homes; and they are more aware of the architectural clichés in American suburbs. One of them said to me:

'When my brother-in-law recently gave his daughter a red Buick convertible for a graduation present, my wife and I thought how a trip abroad would have been a much more lasting gift. A year ago we would have taken the convertible for granted.'

As the course was drawing to its close each of its members was asked to fill out an anonymous questionnaire in which he was to give his opinion of the course and the effect it had had on him. A number of revealing, if not surprising, changes in attitude came to light. Reading habits, for one thing, had changed. 'I'm taking more advantage of library facilities, reading two newspapers, and reviewing several good news magazines,' one man said. Another reported, 'I approach newspapers and periodicals with much more curiosity and speculation than before; politics make more sense; the art section in *Time* is not only readable but interesting; I read the book review section in the *New York Times*; questions concerning McCarthyism are thought through with some real attention to ultimate questions.'

But perhaps more revealing comments were made by the men at a dinner held last May in a private dining room at the Philadelphia Racquet Club where Cleo Craig, the president of the American Telephone and Telegraph Company, was the guest of honor. After the entrée Craig asked each of the men to summarize briefly what he had gotten out of the course. It was evident that the men had primarily learned something about themselves.

'When I first went to work for Bell during the Depression, I spent twelve to fourteen months collecting coin boxes,' one of them said. 'From that time on, I worked all the time and sacrificed everything to get ahead. Now things are different. I still want to get along in the company but I now realize that I owe something to myself, my family, and my community.'

A second man said, 'This course has given me a new interest in my status and my inheritance, and a mode of determining what they are.' Another was 'less content with personal values than before,' and went on to say that the course had 'stimulated a creeping discontent and loss of complacency.' Finally, one of them summed up his feelings about the program as follows: 'Before this course, I was like a straw floating with the current down the stream. The stream was the Bell Telephone Company. I don't think I will ever be like that straw again.'

The men all went back to their jobs in July. Almost six months later, during Christmas week, I talked with seven of them and had long letters from three others. Although the effects of such an educational program as this one cannot be measured with any precision, some interesting effects that it has had on the men are already apparent.

In the first place, it must be remembered they were chosen because of their demonstrated abilities and strong drives towards success in the Bell System. They are, they report, glad to be 'in harness' again, and on the whole they have found the transition back to their jobs much easier than getting used to the program of the Institute. One theme runs through their comments on the effects of the program: they have considerably more confidence in themselves, which, in turn, has 'created an even stronger desire for more and broader responsibility in the business.'

This self-confidence has resulted, they feel, in a greater ability to make decisions: 'I think the chief benefit from the program is a kind of emotional detachment. I don't feel the same personal involvement and emotional insecurity about business problems. This increase in objectivity adds to my confidence in taking the risk of decision. I get more sleep now too!' To find this confidence born of objectivity is all the more gratifying to those of us at the Institute because several of us visualized the successful business executive as someone who 'flew by the seat of his pants,' as the saying goes, and possessed some kind of intuitive 'feel' for the right decision. Well aware of the archetypical intellectual's difficulty in arriving at decisions because of a tendency to see all sides of every question, we were afraid that the Institute's program might educate this intuitive feel out of these promising young men. The following comment seems to me a wise refutation of these fears:

'I have been much more efficient in organizing the relevant facts and placing alternative courses of action in sharp focus. Although I now see more angles and am less sure that any particular decision is *the* right one, I am aided in making it by the realization that there is probably no *one* right solution to many problems. I am now much less upset, and more able to learn, by mistakes.' Another man says of his new sense of perspective and objectivity: 'This may sound contradictory, but I find myself to be much more critical than before and, at the same time, much more tolerant.'

This confidence and assurance evidently has not been limited to their life in business. One man in a large Midwestern city, for example, talked about the Institute to a social club composed of professional people interested in the arts and literature: he was extremely gratified both by their response to his talk and because he got along with them so well in informal conversation afterwards.

These young men of affairs have not *become* intellectuals. They are not bringing bookish ideas from the program into their business and community life: rather, they have developed into sympathetic and informed listeners, or catalysts in drawing out other people's interests. As one writes: 'A particularly well-read person in the company who used to interest me very little has become a fast friend of mine and is fostering my continued interest in ideas unwittingly. I of course do most of the listening.'

Intellectual Know-How

What Americans proudly call 'know-how' has produced many things: great corporations, great bombs, and a great many automobiles and refrigerators. In the Institute of Humanistic Studies for Executives, however, Bell's high managers are seeking to remedy a weakness in American democracy which Tocqueville discerned over one hundred years ago: 'It would seem as if the rulers of our time,' he said, 'sought only to use men in order to make things great; I wish they would try a little more to make great men; that they set less value on the work, and more value upon the workman.'

From the point of view of the Bell System, it is far too early to assess the value of their experiment. But it is perhaps significant that the wives, at the picnic celebrating the completion of the program, provided a large cake with one candle and this inscription:

With Love and Kisses

to

'The Humans'

Class of 1954

---

finishing time

---

speed.........w.p.m. (page 243) comprehension.........(page 134)

SUMMARY

BELL TELEPHONE'S EXPERIMENT

The future policy-makers of the Company were over-special-ized. The firm needed educated rather than trained executives: imaginative men who could ask the questions, not merely answer them.

Seventeen middle executives, mostly college graduates in their thirties, were therefore sent on a ten-month course at the University of Pennsylvania to study humanities and liberal arts: literature (works like Joyce's *Ulysses*), history, art, phil-osophy, sociology, etc. The course proceeded from less familiar to more familiar subjects. There was some resistance at first, but in the end they all became deeply involved in cultural activities.

After they had been back in the firm for some months, they reported that they had more confidence and wanted greater responsibility. They could make better decisions because their attitude was more detached, critical, tolerant, and objective; they could see all sides of a question and realized there was not always one solution. Although they had wider interests, they were still ambitious.

In their private lives they became more interested in ideas and people, without becoming 'intellectuals'. They realized they owed something to themselves and their families as well as to the firm. Their wives were delighted.

The conclusion was that it was far too early for the firm to assess the value of the experiment.

MARKING

We suggest something like the following (the marks are in brackets). You should resist any inclination to interpret the guide summary too literally.

Problem of the firm (1).

15 to 20 young (middle) executives; 9 to 12 months (1).

Some indication of syllabus (1).

Less familiar to more familiar subjects (1).

Some resistance at first, enthusiasm later (1).

Better decisions (1); two other points (2).

If it is implied that the *firm* thought the men had changed, subtract 2.

Broad cultural activities in their private lives (1).

Too early for the firm to assess results (2).

(On this scoring you can drop a point and still get 10.)

Modify the marking scheme if you wish.

Comments

A weakness in the reading of 'problem' passages is that insufficient time is given to the conclusions. The firm did not conclude that the experiment was an unqualified success: the *executives* said they were changed men; it was too early for the firm to say anything. (We understand this method of training was abandoned.)

Many readers go into unnecessary detail and give far too little information about the behaviour of the men when they returned to work. Refer to paragraph six, which gives the ages of the men (eleven between 35 and 40; three in their thirties; and one who was 48); it has often been pointed out to us in summaries that $11 + 3 + 1$ makes 15, not 17 executives. We have the impression that some readers retain facts and only interpret them when they come to write the summaries. Most of the interpretation should be done while the reading is taking place: in this way the reader reads with proper emphasis, understands far more easily and accurately, and spares himself the tremendous effort of trying to remember a multitude of facts; if he delays his comprehension, he is not likely to comprehend at all and will soon forget what he has read; what is more, subsequent interpretation may distort the meaning, because of the reader's interests and attitudes. The reading of two newspapers, for example, was not one of the main reactions to the experiment: it was the experience of *one* man, quoted among other examples to show how reading habits in the widest sense had changed. Again, it cannot be inferred that the men got more sleep – a favourite with readers who are themselves executives – though *one* man certainly did.

This passage could, of course, be read in different ways for different purposes: fast for the unembroidered facts or more slowly for the full account; but whatever the purpose there is every reason for anticipating the structure of the article and requiring answers to questions, because this is good, active reading which improves comprehension.

Suggestions for Practice

Choose several short articles. Follow the suggestions for previewing that are given on page 49: when you have finished previewing, spend a minute or two trying to anticipate the topic. You should also practise anticipation without previewing.

CHAPTER 8

ORGANIZATION

BY organization we mean the general arrangement of a piece of writing – its skeleton. Organization is a matter of degree; in a sense every word is part of the 'whole' organization. We are only concerned with the skeleton, because attention to this can sometimes make all the difference between quick, easy reading and slow, difficult plodding. Attention to the skeleton is appropriate in circumstances like these:

When the skeleton is on the outside, as in scientific writing. Business reports are usually organized in this way.

When the author feels it necessary to expose parts of the skeleton. If the reader ignores these helpful indications, his intuitive awareness of the hidden parts of the skeleton may fail him.

When the skeleton conforms to a type, so that it can be inferred, even though it is concealed.

When the reader needs to read selectively. The skeleton can help him to limit his reading and locate his objective.

When the author's skeleton is not what it should be. There must be some skeletal organization, or the writing would be incomprehensible. But it does not follow that badly organized writing cannot be fully comprehended; it can if the ideas are there; but it is hard work reorganizing a going concern like a piece of writing.

Readers often ask: 'Why doesn't the author give us more help?' They want synopses, summaries, headings, subheadings, lots of italics, and paragraphs headed by 'topic' sentences. This raises a fundamental question of how writing is organized. We shall examine the principles of organization, giving reasons for exposing or not exposing the skeleton. Then we shall indicate certain main types of skeleton that can be easily recognized. Finally, we shall consider the skill that is required of the reader.

How Writing is Organized

This is a question of Science and Art. The purpose of science is knowledge. The scientist makes no appeal: he states his case and shows how he states it. The skeleton is always on the outside: the organization of the writing is *external*. Art, on the other hand, is personal. The artist appeals to the imagination; the skeleton does not protrude. The organization of the writing is *internal*, except for the title, and sometimes the chapter headings. Between those two extremes, varying amounts of skeleton are exposed: the more knowledge there is, the more the skeleton is *exposed*; the more art there is, the more the skeleton is *concealed*.

Writing, even at its most informative, is largely an art, because it must appeal to the reader's interest and stimulate his imagination. The author who writes for the general reader always has the problem of how much skeleton to reveal for the sake of clarity; if he helps the reader too much, his work looks, and reads, like a scientific tract: the reader who sees a skull may get the impression there is too much pure knowledge for his liking and fight shy.

Familiar Types of Organization

The classic exposition of the way writing is organized is the *Explication de Texte,* so dear to the French. The essence of this is the consideration of the whole in relation to the parts, the parts in relation to the whole, and the movement of the whole. The method is elaborated with great subtlety: a wonderful discipline for the writer and an excellent tool for critical analysis; but the reader would never submit his everyday reading to such close scrutiny, and there is no reason why he should. A perfectly easy piece of writing may have a most intricate structure, while the general plan of difficult ideas may be simplicity itself. Our concern is not the grammar of organization, but a practical, working approach to ordinary, everyday reading. We shall, however, not lose sight of the *Explication de Texte*, because its approach can help us.

Let us consider the two basic activities: investigating and explaining. When either activity is fairly distinct, and not inextricably bound up with the other, then the skeleton of the written presentation can, as a rule, be easily discerned or inferred, even when the writer has embodied it completely.

1. INVESTIGATING

One familiar type of organization is PROBLEM – DISCUSSION – CONCLUSIONS. Here, the logical *movement* is so powerful that the organization is usually internal, except in the case of business or scientific reports, when prescribed headings are used for additional clarity and quick reference. The Bell Telephone article, a popular account of a social experiment, was an example of investigating in such a pure form that it was possible to anticipate the general arrangement and read for answers to specific questions. Whatever the variations and elaborations, there is a logical movement, which dominates the organization of the material. Whenever a problem is tackled outright, and not introduced to express a mood of questioning, exploration, or qualification, the reader can expect to find a route leading to a destination – the conclusions. We have observed from readers' summaries that the conclusions are often read too fast: either with no reduction in speed or even with an 'end-spurt'.

Investigating may start with the facts and take these forms: FACTS – ANALYSIS – CONCLUSIONS; or FACTS – ANALYSIS – STATEMENT OF PROBLEM; or FACTS – ANALYSIS – PROBLEM – DISCUSSION – CONCLUSIONS. Again, the movement is so powerful that the reader usually requires no additional help from the author by way of formal headings. It is, of course, an advantage if he can anticipate the general organization; but whether he does so or not, he has only to grasp the meaning to be carried along by the movement. A variation of these latter types of organization is AREAS OF INVESTIGATION – IMPLICATIONS AND ANALYSIS – CONCLUSIONS. There is a fundamental psychological process by which meaning is discovered: ideas are grouped according to their affinities and characteristics; which makes it possible to see implications and arrive at new meanings. When information is grouped in this way, the reader is often provided in advance with an outline or plan to show how the parts are arranged. Grouping, however, may occur in *any* type of organization and at any stage; for example: PROBLEM – AREAS OF DISCUSSION – CONCLUSIONS; and when this is so, the reader should be on the alert for outlines and pointers; indications of this kind are always the occasion for slower reading.

2. EXPLAINING

In this kind of activity the emphasis is on the whole in relation to the parts. Here are some examples. The author may describe characteristics, aspects, qualities: AND THIS, AND THIS. He may explain an operation, a process or a procedure: DO THIS, THEN THIS. He may narrate: AND THEN, AND THEN. He may give his reasons or unfold an argument: BECAUSE OF THIS, THEN THIS. Whatever his organization, there are always steps, stages, phases, aspects, areas, periods, divisions – in fact, *parts*.

The problem for both author and reader is to bind these parts into a whole. The parts are not equally important and there may be much incidental description, explanation, and illustration to drive the main points home; so the reader must be selective; but he cannot miss an important point or the whole will collapse. To ensure the understanding of the whole, the author may make introductory comments on scope, purpose, and methods; he may give an outline of the whole or describe the main features; he may summarize or emphasize as he goes; and he may provide a final summary or 'conclusion'. (In this connexion the conclusion does not announce the destination, for the destination is the whole; 'in conclusion' can mean almost anything: the last point, a summary, general observations, or a leave-taking.)

When this activity exists in a relatively pure form, then there must be a framework; this is not difficult to discern and the reader usually gets the help he requires; but he has to be on the alert.

Investigating and explaining are often inextricably involved one with the other: in which case the skeleton is a general arrangement that varies from passage to passage. If the reader grasps the main points, the organization is implicit in his understanding, even though he may not be aware of it.

What the Reader Should Do

1. Learn to recognize at a glance the habitual linguistic and typographical signposts of organization.

2. Learn to recognize distinct investigating and explaining types of organization.

3. Whenever there is evidence of grouping, watch very closely for introductory outlines and for summaries.

4. Cultivate a general awareness of organization and of how different kinds of writing tend to conform to different patterns: for example, how book reviews often contain their recommendations in the last line or two; and how news reports usually arrange the information in order of importance or news value.

What to Do Next

The next exercise, 'Contract for the Design and Development of a Wireless Set', is a report by the Committee of Public Accounts. It is not a passage for fast reading, as normally it would be read several times; efficiency must therefore be the criterion: the saving of time and effort.

The method of reading a report depends on the nature of the material and the reader's individual technique. As an *exercise* you will be asked to read this passage several times in prescribed ways; which is not the only method; nor is it the method you yourself would necessarily adopt. You will obtain your speed in relation to your total time for the various readings; provided your comprehension is satisfactory, 200–250 w.p.m. is very efficient; 250–350 w.p.m., highly efficient; and 350–450 w.p.m., remarkably so – only a few readers can achieve this.

PROCEDURE

The purpose is a general understanding. Turn over the pages to get a total impression: you will see at a glance that it is a short, compact statement with no headings; you can therefore confidently anticipate a straightforward report of the type: PROBLEM – DISCUSSION – CONCLUSIONS – RECOMMENDATIONS. This determines the method of reading.

1. *Previewing.* Read (do not skim) the first and last *paragraphs,* and the first *sentences* of the remaining paragraphs. The time for previewing must be included in your total reading time.

2. *Reading.* When you have finished previewing, start reading immediately, using your judgement about the way you cover the parts of the text you have already read.

3. *Reviewing.* As soon as you have finished reading, skim over the passage to verify, clarify and emphasize. (Do not attempt to remember detailed information, such as figures or dates.) The time for reviewing must be included in your total reading time.

4. Write a summary: 270 words at the outside.

5. Mark your summary by referring to the guide summary and marking scheme that follow immediately after the reading passage.

Exercise 13   (1320 words)

THIRD REPORT FROM THE COMMITTEE
OF PUBLIC ACCOUNTS 1961–62*
Paragraphs 62 to 69, concerning the

CONTRACT FOR THE DESIGN AND
DEVELOPMENT OF A WIRELESS SET

starting time

62. In March, 1960, the Ministry of Aviation sought competitive tenders from eight firms for the development and produc-

* Reproduced by permission of H.M. Stationery Office.

tion of a new type of wireless set of which about 600 were required for the Army by 1965. The firms were invited to attend a meeting at which they were given information on general and technical questions before returning tenders. They were told at this meeting that it would be helpful if they submitted technical appreciations of the task to be undertaken, although such appreciations were not called for in the tender documents. Tenders were received from all the eight firms, and technical appreciations were submitted by six firms, in April, 1960.

63. When the tenders were first considered early in May, 1960, the Ministry's Technical Branch recommended that the contract should be placed with a particular firm who had quoted the highest price for development and the second highest overall price for development and production. One of the grounds for this recommendation was the superiority of this firm's technical appreciation. Four firms were subsequently short-listed – the successful firm, who had offered delivery in 1964, and three others, offering delivery in 1963. One of these three was the lowest tenderer, whose overall price for development and production was less than one-half of that of the successful firm, partly because they were prepared to accept a development price representing only a small proportion of their estimate of development costs. The Ministry submitted this short list to the War Office, but stated that in their opinion the firms other than the successful firm, though less costly, would not be likely to meet their delivery dates and might not be able to begin production until 1966. The War Office were unable to accept this risk, and the contract was accordingly placed with the successful firm in October, 1960, after they had agreed to some reduction in price. The reduction, amounting to approximately 20 per cent. overall on their original tender price, left the price to be paid still considerably in excess of those quoted by the lowest and several of the other tenderers.

64. Your Committee cannot escape the conclusion that resort by the Ministry to competitive tender completely failed in its purpose in this case. The contract was stated to be the first attempt by the Ministry in the communications field to place a

major development contract following competitive tender, in furtherance of their policy of placing fixed price contracts wherever possible. The Ministry explained that it was in the nature of a pilot experiment; the possibility of substantial orders outside the United Kingdom providing an incentive for manufacturers to compete for the contract. Your Committee welcome this initiative. The advantages of fixed price contracts are clear, and competitive tender provides the most satisfactory basis by which fixed prices may be established. Your Committee are satisfied that the Ministry were right in seeking competition for this order. They recommend that, nothwithstanding the difficulties presented by the special nature of development work, the Ministry should do all they can to foster competition in this field. Every effort should, however, be made to ensure that the conditions of tendering are so devised as to make the competition effective.

65. In the first place, where the nature of the work to be done makes it necessary for tendering to be restricted to a limited number of firms, it is perhaps self-evident that invitations to tender should not be issued to firms whose tenders are likely to be rejected on extraneous grounds. Doubts about the capability of any particular firm to undertake the work concerned, unless likely to be resolved by the tender itself, constitute a reason for omission from the tender list in the first place as much as for rejection of the subsequent tender. In the case under review the Ministry explained that they were not certain which firms could produce the kind of wireless set required and they were concerned at the outset to exclude firms not able to do so. Your Committee noted, however, that an important factor in the rejection of one tender was stated to be the poor performance of the firm on an earlier contract, and the extent to which they had required supervision and help from the Ministry. While Your Committee accept the Ministry's explanation that this was only one factor in the rejection, and that the technical appreciation submitted by this firm had been inadequate, they would point out that this only serves to emphasise the importance of the second requirement to which they now wish to draw attention.

66. The second requirement is that all tenders should be rendered and judged on an identical basis, and tenderers should be left in no doubt as to what information is required, and on what basis their tenders are to be assessed. The outcome of the tendering for the wireless set makes it quite clear that price alone, without reference to the merit of the technical appreciation, was not a governing factor in the award of that contract. Yet the tender documents did not state that such an appreciation was required. The tenderers were merely told informally that appreciations would be helpful, and, while six firms did in fact submit them, Your Committee remain in some doubt whether they were aware of the overriding importance of this requirement, or even of the precise nature or comprehensiveness of the appreciation called for.

67. Thirdly, where time of completion is likely to be a material factor in the award of a contract, tenderers should be required to indicate in the fullest detail possible the progress, stage by stage, which they aim at achieving, with the clear understanding that such a timescale will be written into and become part of the contract. The firms tendering for the wireless set were told that time was of the essence of the contract, but the issue of how they would space out development was left to them. The Ministry then refused to rely on the completion dates offered by the firms and based the award of the contract on the estimates made by technical officers of the Ministry of the time likely to be taken by the various tenderers. Your Committee are clear that this was a faulty procedure and that it did not establish beyond reasonable doubt that firms which had been prepared to undertake the work at less cost than the successful firm and complete it earlier would not have been able to do so.

68. Finally, the financial advantage of a fixed price contract will be dissipated if subsequently the Ministry make alterations in the contract conditions or in the nature of the work to be done. Shortly after the award of the contract for the wireless set the contractor was informed that he was to take over the function of Design Authority from the Ministry's Signals Research and Development Establishment, and that it was desired

to proceed to a revised specification. Both these changes entailed revision of the contract price. Your Committee do not wish to comment on the necessity or otherwise of these changes. It seems to them, however, that alterations of this nature cannot fail to militate against the achievement of a competitive fixed price.

69. Your Committee are of the opinion that in the award of the contract for the wireless set technical convenience was allowed to prevail over other considerations, to the extent that in this case competitive tendering proved to be a farce. They are satisfied that competition has an important part to play in the field of development. But it is essential that competition should be properly organised, and that technical convenience should not be allowed to outweigh broader considerations of financial advantage and the wider distribution in industry of capacity to meet Service requirements. They recommend that the Ministry should review their procedure in the light of the principles enunciated above.

---

finishing time

---

speed......w.p.m. (page 242) comprehension...... (pages 146–7)

SUMMARY (EXERCISE 13)

CONTRACT FOR WIRELESS SETS

Problem

The Ministry of Aviation invited tenders for the development and production of wireless sets. The contract was awarded to the firm with the highest price for development and the second highest price for development and production. The reasons for this were the superiority of the firm's technical appreciation and the Ministry's decision that it could not rely on the delivery dates of the other firms.

Discussion

1. A firm with a poor record was not excluded from the tender list.

146

2. Tenders were not assessed on an identical basis, because a technical appreciation, though mentioned, was not formally specified.

3. Time was an essential factor, but firms were not asked for stage-by-stage schedules.

4. The Ministry subsequently altered the conditions of the contract and lost the advantages of a fixed price.

Conclusions and Recommendations

Technical convenience decided the award and competitive tendering was a farce.

Competitive tendering is advantageous and should be encouraged; apart from the financial advantages, it gives a wider distribution of industrial capacity to meet Service requirements.

The Ministry's procedures were not properly organized and should be reviewed in the light of the four main criticisms.

MARKING

This is a rough guide (the marks are in brackets): *Problem* (3) – high-cost firm (1); reasons (2). *Discussion* (4). *Conclusions and Recommendations* (4). (This gives a bonus of one mark.)

The marks should be distributed according to the form of the summary, which is unlikely to be the same as the example we have provided.

Comments

From the preview we get some idea of the problem: the contract was awarded to a high-cost firm for reasons of technical convenience, although technical appreciations were not called for; we also learn the four grounds for criticism, and the conclusions and recommendations. In the final skimming we are able to bring the ideas into sharp focus and concentrate on points that need more attention if they are to be retained. Had we needed the information 'highest price for development and second highest price for development and production' this could have been extracted during the final skimming: slow reading is usually not slow enough for this kind of detail and can be surprisingly inaccurate.

We suggest that when this report came into the hands of those concerned, the preliminary stages of reading might have been somewhat along the lines of the exercise. The need to understand the Committee's 'whole' thought would have led straight to the conclusions and recommendations; and the grounds for criticism might then have been taken at speed in reverse order, because 'Finally', 'Thirdly', 'The second require-ment', and 'In the first place', could scarcely have failed to attract attention, drawing the eye upwards from the bottom of the page. The first reading would probably have been fast, fol-lowed perhaps by skimming to locate specific items for close scrutiny. Ultimately, every word would have been weighed by repeated readings.

In urgent, practical situations the reader seems to obey quite spontaneously what are called 'laws' of learning, moving when-ever possible from the general to the particular, learning in *phases* instead of piecemeal, allowing the schemas to form organically by a constructive process of repetition and integra-tion. (We shall return to this when we consider the reading of books, in Chapter 11.)

Suggestions for Practice

Preview, read, and *review* a few longer articles, testing your comprehension by means of summaries. Exercises of this kind, apart from anything else, increase one's awareness of how writing is organized.

CHAPTER 9

ATTITUDES

Judgement, Bias, and Prejudice

ATTITUDES exert a powerful influence on the way we read and comprehend. This is not widely recognized; and even readers who appreciate the significance of attitudes for other forms of communication sometimes have an attitude to reading that makes them treat it as though it were a neutral activity.

We comprehend by a process of selection and organization. This is not the work of a thinking machine, but of a person with hopes, fears, preferences, and attitudes. The way we select our facts and organize our minds, the way we think, depends on our judgement – our values and whole attitude to life. As Charles Darwin wrote: 'All observation must be for or against some view.' Reading is not the comprehension of cut-and-dried information: it is the agreement or disagreement of the points of view of an author and a reader.

All judgement has a natural bias in the sense that it is a *vision* of life: the truth as we see it after due consideration of the facts. But when judgements are made without considering the facts, our thinking is prejudiced. Prejudices are usually habitual. Contrary to the popular view, they are not always harmful; nor are they invariably hostile to the truth; because many of our attitudes are the result of instinctive feelings. Allied to the reader's natural bias, there is often an element of prejudice, which may or may not be harmful or hostile. When considering the influence of attitudes on reading, we need to exercise caution and, above all, be tolerant.

The Author's Tone

Tone is a persuasive quality of the text: the author's general attitude and the overflow of his personality. In the *Explication de Texte*, of which we spoke in the last chapter, the reader is enjoined to consider the author's '*angoisses*' and '*passions*' and his tone. When the reader is aware of the tone of the writing, he can often anticipate not only the author's general approach but his attitude to particular issues. The author's judgement, whether or not it is prejudiced, is usually of a piece, consistent with itself and with his whole attitude and personality; and to be aware of his tone is to understand his personality, his attitude, his way of thinking – his judgement. Sensitivity to tone increases the reader's powers of anticipation, helps him to read more actively and improves his comprehension.

In the reading of informative material, this awareness of tone is enhanced if there is no unnecessary attention to details; for the reader cannot be wholly responsive unless his effort is properly distributed. But other kinds of literature, such as novels, are a different matter; where tone is created by detailed observation, there may be scope for variations in pace, but less opportunity, in our opinion, for fast, flexible reading.

The Reader's Attitudes

Readers are inclined to see what they believe. This is natural enough, because new experience must always be related to existing patterns of thought and behaviour. Readers on our courses who have analysed their answers to the comprehension questions tell us that their mistakes are often due to understanding what they thought the author *should* have said.

Readers, moreover, are disposed to believe what they would like to believe and to ignore anything that does not conform to their own attitudes. This, again, is not unnatural, because readers have to preserve the stability of their experience. One of the authors of this book used to discuss problems of communication with groups of foremen and got to know one group particularly well. A written statement was prepared containing *some* of the things they evidently liked about their work and *all* the things they seemed to dislike. A foreman was asked to read this and then write down what he had remembered; his statement was passed to another foreman and the procedure repeated until the last foreman had his statement: it contained all the things they liked about their work that were in the original statement as well as other things they liked that had been deliberately excluded; but most of the things they disliked had been forgotten. These men were extremely tolerant and understanding; and the example is not given in any spirit of criticism; it is meant to illustrate what happens to us all. Attitudes are far more powerful and selective than readers imagine.

Emotions and enthusiasms, which stimulate active, imaginative reading, strengthen our attitudes and are, therefore, not without their dangers. A reading passage we use on our courses contains the expression 'Humour is akin to religion', and some readers, for whom these are highly emotive words, respond by ignoring the author's tone and interpreting the article, quite mistakenly, as though religion were the main theme. Even the most discerning readers make mistakes like this.

There are also emotions and attitudes of a different kind. Some readers are completely thrown by American spelling, let alone American expressions (by American authors). Others are disdainful of 'literature', 'journalism', 'light reading', or 'old-fashioned styles'; and are predisposed to show hostility. Some readers find it difficult to understand anything they disagree with; they fight the author and become insensitive to his tone and meaning.

Reading as a Personal Relationship

As readers, we must accept the fact of our bias; it is part of our personality and attitude to life. Prejudices that are hostile to the truth are, for the most part, by their very nature, blind; and there is little we can do about them in our reading – at least, directly. The advice, 'watch your attitudes', sometimes seems to imply that all bias and prejudice are bad and should be avoided, which is not the case; or that prejudice that is hostile to the truth can be eliminated by an act of will, which is extremely doubtful, because we seldom recognize such prejudice in ourselves.

What, then, can the reader do? Perhaps only this: accept

reading for what it is, a relationship; and observe the essential condition of any personal relationship, which is to understand the other in his own terms. If, as readers, we accept the fact of our natural bias; if we assume that we have all manner of prejudices, both good and bad; if we recognize that misunderstandings on our part are to some extent inevitable; then we are more likely to understand the author in his own terms, to be tolerant of his attitudes, and to welcome the challenge of ideas that are not our own. By adopting this attitude to reading, we learn about ourselves; for reading is not something apart from life. We read as we live – tolerantly or intolerantly; but it is also true to say that we live as we read.

What to Do Next

Before doing the next exercise, write against each of the following words a reminder of the first few ideas that come freely to mind; the less conscious effort you make, the better. (We shall refer to this later.)

THE ESTABLISHMENT:

THE CHURCH:

TRADITION:

MATERIAL PROGRESS:

KITCHEN-SINK PLAYS:

TELEVISION SATIRISTS:

Previewing and Reading (the next two passages)

Write down your starting time and preview for as long as you think necessary; when you have finished previewing, do not pause, but start reading. (*Your total time will therefore include your previewing time.*)

Comprehension

Both passages have multiple-choice questions.

Exercise 14   (1520 words)

ANTIDISESTABLISHMENTARIANISM*

by Àlan Brien – *Queen*, March 1963

starting time

Whether or not that is the longest word in the English language, it is certainly the most enduring ism in English history. Antidisestablishmentarianism was coined in the 19th century to describe the body of opinion which opposed the separation of Church and State. It is equally appropriate to describe the body of opinion which opposes the separation of the upper classes and the State. I do not wish to attempt an analysis of the Establishment now. Nobody who has lived for more than a year in this country can doubt that it throws its shadow over every activity of the Queen's subjects. Like the dark side of the moon, it has still never been fully mapped. Like the dark side of the moon, it is there whether we can see it or not. It is sufficient to say, in George Orwell's phrase, that 'we are a family with the wrong members in control'. The most efficient way of identifying an Establishmentarian is to test him with two questions. Does he (a) make the rules, and (b) break them? The rules may be laws of the land, customs of the clan, etiquette of the house, traditions of the school, habits of the class, fashions of the day, or regulations of grammar. But one thing is certain

* Reproduced by permission of the editor of *Queen*.

– the Establishmentarian will ensure that they are binding upon everyone else but him. The more he embodies their values in public and defies them in private, the nearer he will be to the top brick in the pyramid.

He passes the Licensing Acts for pubs and ignores them in his clubs. He owns newspapers which invade the privacy of people he does not know, but he makes sure that his own privacy is protected even by his rival press lords. He supports the monarchy as a principle, but makes fun of members of the Royal Family in practice. He loves horses and denounces those who ill-treat dogs from the magistrates' bench, but he shoots down birds by the thousand and regrets the shortage of foxes to hunt. He upholds the sanctity of marriage and the holiness of the family, but has been twice divorced and sends his children away to boarding school at the age of seven. His motto is 'A place for everybody and everybody in his place'.

Just how aware the Establishmentarian is of these contradictions and inconsistencies I find it hard to be certain. Our era has attracted many labels. It has been called the Age of Anxiety, of Agnosticism, of the Status Symbol, of the Manipulators. All have some justification, but perhaps more than any other this is the Age of Self-consciousness. Never before have so many people been fascinated by the sight of their own faces.

The mystic fogs which once shrouded almost all the workings of society are being rapidly burned off. Psychologists, sociologists, economists, market researchers and pollsters feed us an endless flow of information about ourselves. In novels and in White Papers, in television serials and in newspaper investigations, in statistics and in charts, we are told what we eat, how we will vote, why we buy, when we go to bed, where we spend our holidays and whether we are likely to die of cancer or of coronary thrombosis. The accident no longer exists. Every act has both an end and an origin. No longer could a new Irish famine, a second Depression, or a Third World War be regarded simply as an Act of God.

The Establishment is the last of the forbidden temples in an unknown land – the Tibet of social geography. And Antidisestablishmentarianism is the religion of its guardians. The high priests of the top people still have enough incense in the censers to keep up a smoke screen. One method of veiling the Established altar is to pretend that the Establishment no longer exists. Even the word itself has been carefully eroded by over-exposure. It has become a cliché, a joke, an old-fashioned bogey name, the title of a night club. Those who write about it are patronisingly advised that it is as outmoded in sociology as the phlogiston theory is in chemistry.

Another device of Antidisestablishmentarianism is the display of mascots. It is possible to make a career out of being the insider's outsider – the one Jew in the golf club, the one grammar schoolboy in the Cabinet, the one Communist at High Table, the one radical columnist on the Tory newspaper, the one atheist TV producer, the one Labour millionaire.

When medieval kings went into battle, they scattered their ranks with pseudo-kings wearing imitation crowns to confuse the enemy sharpshooters. Just so do the Antidisestablishment-arians create a dozen masks of the Establishment and spur the hunters on to exhaust themselves pursuing the fake quarry. The most publicised evils of society are always those which are most popular among the masses and least important to the few. Bingo, the football pools, teddy boys, illegitimacy, teenage sex, television, shop stewards, betting shops, materialism – these are set up as Aunt Sallies to distract the critics from the real targets. The favourite scapegoat of the professional moralists at the moment is the trades union. Perhaps the most conservative force in British politics, the mainstay and anchor of right wing in the Labour Party for generations, they are continually daubed as the fortress of subversion. Even such a clear-sighted and experienced observer as Arthur Koestler was recently misled by this red herring into claiming that the greatest danger to the British way of life lay in the infiltration of the unions by Communists.

The Establishment stands to gain most by the *status quo* – or .perhaps it should be renamed the *status quid*. It needs society to be a stationary machine, a beached Rolls stuck in the mud. As long as the engine purrs on, keeping the lights bright and the heater warm, it will be cosy inside even if the wheels are slipping. And so, by luck or design, they have arranged an ingenious negative feedback in the fuel system.

Whenever the mixture gets too rich and there is a danger that the vehicle may begin to move, a cut-off device ensures that the fuel bypasses the cylinders and cannot explode. The Establishmentarians then announce that disaster has been avoided by a hair's breadth and call on the rest of the nation to start pushing.

This charade has preserved the British hierarchical system again and again. It is at present being played out once more. This is the essence of Antidisestablishmentarianism and it works through a kind of black propaganda which makes its enemies over-complacent by exaggerating their victories. As soon as the first signs of tiny rebellion appear, the Establishment stages a mass counter-attack crying 'backs to the wall'. They mow down their critics shouting 'We surrender'.

Examples are almost too many and too obvious to list. For the last six months, all but two or three of London's 35 theatres have been occupied by musicals, comedies and thrillers. As I write, only one houses a new straight play – *The Tulip Tree*, a weepy middle-class soap opera full of sentimental defeatism, by N. C. Hunter. Yet hardly a week passes without some peer or prelate or leader-writer or impresario complaining that our stage is infested with kitchen-sink propaganda full of four-letter words.

In five years the British film industry has taken time off from mass-producing genteel Ealing comedies, seaside postcard farces, stiff upper-lip submarine melodramas and American-backed epics to allow a handful of young writers and directors to show the working class without patronage. Films like *Room at the Top*, *Look Back in Anger*, *A Taste of Honey*, *Saturday Night and Sunday Morning* and *This Sporting Life* represent a tiny proportion of the Wardour Street output. Yet to listen to television discussions and read newspaper pundits, you would imagine that our cinema screens displayed nothing but pregnant mill girls and vomiting lathe operators.

The teaching of English in our universities, especially in the Establishment citadels of Oxford and Cambridge, is still dominated by dried-up philologists, editors of minor works of minor authors, and half a dozen romantic enthusers who taste books like a wine snob tastes vintages. Yet our literary weeklies and Sunday paper dilettantes still announce with mock resignation that Dr. F. R. Leavis and his disciples hold the undergraduate youth of Britain in thrall and dissect our literature coldly under an anaesthetic. The truth is that Dr. Leavis recently retired from Downing College having never occupied any position more influential than that of Reader, and his magazine *Scrutiny*, the best work of enlightened scholarship ever published in this country, ceased publication many years ago. Leavis's nearest rival, F. R. Bateson at Oxford, is simply a Lecturer and has never been made a Fellow of his own college.

The Government's slogan today seems to be 'You never should have had it so good'. From all the taps in the Establishment communication system comes a constant drip of rebuke directed at the Coronation Street playboys, the public bar fast set, and the New Town bright young things who are turning the working-class areas of Britain into gilded playgrounds. It is seriously alleged that the backbone of the nation, stiffened in the Depression, is going weak in the marrow through an over-indulgence in motor cars, washing machines, continental holidays and tailor-made suits. Inconvenient evidence, such as the fact that half of our houses have no bathrooms and a disgracefully large minority have no separate lavatory, is simply ignored.

The negative feedback is always hard at work discrediting the satirical accuracy of a programme like *That Was The Week That Was* or a magazine like *Private Eye*. As Antidisestablishmentarianism has so many mouths, it does not have to concern itself about consistency. One pair of lips whispers that these callow youngsters are pointlessly cruel, frivolously destructive and schoolboyishly silly. Another larynx chuckles that they are just harmless jesters and indulgent kidders whose gibes bounce off their victims with no ill-feeling on either side. Even such bona-fide critics of society as Colin MacInnes, Michael Frayn and Kenneth Tynan have been side-tracked into denouncing the new satirists for minor failings without apparently realising that they are playing the Establishment game.

The result is that 'satire' has become almost as hollow a word as 'Establishment' itself. Whom the gods of the top people would destroy, they first make *à la mode*. Once a concept or an attitude can be tagged as fashionable, it is well on its way to becoming old hat. We are all so hip these days that we begin to wonder if the real hipster is not the square. The black propaganda is on the verge of success once again. The Establishment is posing as the underdog, and we are tempted to feed the hand which bites us.

---

finishing time

QUESTIONS

1 The author describes Antidisestablishmentarianism in its modern form as a body of opinion which (a) opposes progressive ideas; (b) opposes the separation of Church and State; (c) believes in a class society and equality before God; (d) opposes the separation of the upper classes and the State. (   )

2 The Establishmentarian is said to be one who (a) accepts the values of the Church; (b) lives strictly by the prevailing codes of the upper classes; (c) makes the rules and breaks them; (d) believes that there is a natural order of right conduct. (   )

3 More than any other this is (a) the Age of Revolution; (b) the Age of Self-consciousness; (c) the Age of Materialism; (d) the Age of the Manipulators. (   )

4 According to the author, the Establishment protects itself by pretending that it (a) no longer exists; (b) changes with the times; (c) is a democratic élite; (d) is the collective common sense. (   )

5 Another way in which the Establishment protects itself is by (a) appealing to the glories of the past; (b) concentrating on evils which are most popular among the masses, but unimportant to the few; (c)

maintaining a tradition of loyal incorruptible service to the community; (d) giving everyone an opportunity to rise to the top.   ( )

6   The author believes that the enemies of the Establishment become over-complacent because (a) material progress has obscured moral issues; (b) the Left has no philosophy of freedom and is more susceptible to place-seeking, privilege, and restriction than the Right; (c) the victories of reformers are real and progress is being made; (d) the Establishment has a flair for exaggerating the small victories of its opponents.   ( )

7   According to the text, which of the following propositions is true? (a) Films like *Look Back in Anger* represent a large proportion of the Wardour-Street output; (b) kitchen-sink plays occupy most of the London theatres; (c) the enlightened teaching of English in our universities is the best hope of the future: (d) the new movements in drama, films, and literary criticism are a tiny proportion of the whole and are under constant fire.   ( )

8   The Establishment, we are told, seriously alleges that (a) we are weakening from over-indulgence in material things; (b) Britain's strength lies in a healthy regard for class distinction; (c) morality does not require us to share our misery; (d) the British way of life is to level up, not down.   ( )

9   The author considers that the reaction of the Establishment to the new satirists is (a) to regard them as indulgent kidders and pretend there is no ill feeling on either side; (b) to protest that they are frivolously destructive and schoolboyishly silly; (c) to discredit their satiric accuracy by denouncing them with many voices and without regard for consistency; (d) to keep mum and rely on the bona-fide critics to do their work for them.   ( )

10   The author concludes that the propaganda of the Establishment is on the verge of success, because its

method is (a) to tag its critics as dangerous extremists; (b) to pose as the underdog and make reforming
attitudes fashionable; (c) to protest that critical attitudes are not constructive; (d) to lay claim to the
wisdom of the ages.   (   )

speed.........w.p.m. (page 242) comprehension.........(page 235)

Comments

This passage has such a distinctive tone that the skilled reader
would have little difficulty in anticipating the author's approach;
in question 6, for example, (a), (b), and (c) are out of character.

If any of your answers do not agree with the KEY, examine
them in relation to the ideas you associated with the list of
words on page 152). Attitudes, so readers tell us, account for a
fair proportion of the mistakes that are made in comprehension tests. In this test, for example, if question 7 has been
answered incorrectly by a reader who has an aversion to
kitchen-sink plays and who is not a theatre-goer, then the
chances are that he will have selected (b).

Exercise 15   (1060 words)

PUBLIC OPINION

Extract from the Haldane Memorial Lecture 'Formation of
Public Opinion'*
by Sir William Haley – Birkbeck College, March 1958

starting time

What are our hopes and fears for the future? We rightly pride
ourselves on being politically a very old, and on the whole, a
rather wise, race. We rely deep down on the common sense of
the common people. So far it has rarely failed us for long. It

* Reproduced by permission of the author and of the Master of
Birkbeck College.

has shown the world that even abrupt change can be made without violence. It has established authority through institutions while preserving the power to upset them if they become oppressors. It is quick to smell out injustice; zealous against privilege. There can be no country in which the famous 'hate sessions' or other excesses of *Nineteen Eighty-Four* seem less likely to come about.

Yet having assured ourselves of all this, it is a good exercise to define the rights of Public Opinion in terms of four freedoms, and then to ask ourselves if they are all inviolate. I would list them as

Freedom of information.
Freedom of dissent.
Freedom from victimization.
Freedom to exert influence.

Each one of them is, I think, being slowly and subtly threatened.

Freedom of Information

In almost every public activity there are good and responsible people who for (to themselves) good and (again to themselves) responsible reasons believe it is not good for the public to know too much. Often the public seem to acquiesce in the proposition. Newspapers, Delane once declared, live for disclosure. To-day there are all too many facts 'which might be misunderstood.' It is all right to give news to one place but not to another. The proposition is challenged even in responsible quarters that it is always in the highest public interest to tell the truth. Both public and private bodies seem more and more to wish to cloak their proceedings and to present accomplished facts only.

Freedom of Dissent

The need to re-state the doctrine of Mill's *On Liberty* will never grow less. In his day the rights of the minority had to be asserted against the ruling few. Today the enemy that has to be kept at bay is the multitude. The public instinct to suppress uncomfortable opinion is too often under-estimated. It is things to be taken off the air or to be kept out of the newspapers that people at large want. Rarely is the demand – unless it be from interested parties – for the other side to be given.

Freedom from Victimization

Can we say that in this so-called free society every man can be uninhibited about expressing his opinions? From the M.P. who may lose his candidature at the next election if he deflects from the Party line, to the trade unionist who will be sent to Coventry if his conscience does not allow him to obey his fellows' convictions, to the writer who may lose his platforms if he says something unpopular, there is a long line of pressure to enforce the orthodox. We shall be told this is a free country and bodies can act in this way if they wish. They can. But we have not liberty in Mill's sense of the word if they do.

Freedom to Exert Influence

Well, we all know the technique of the politicians who assure interests likely to be affected by their actions that any public raising of the issue will only make things worse. They are always on the point of doing the best thing possible for the interests concerned, if only those interests will not seek the support of public opinion. There are those who hold that *The Times*, being a great national institution, should not express strong views if there is a really sharp national cleavage of opinion. All too often members of public boards, officials, and others have to stay most silent when their own cause is at stake. Some papers suffered appreciably for their advocacy against the Suez adventure. The mumbo-jumbo words 'sub judice' are applied to all kinds of proceedings which are not in the remotest way legal, in order to stifle any expression of opinion about them.

It may be objected that in all this there is nothing new, that it is merely the modern way of defending privilege. I agree. But in the old days there was the most widespread, violent, and healthy reaction against these things. Now that the circle of their perpetration has so immeasurably widened they seem increasingly to be met with acquiescence or apathy.

If it be further objected by anyone here that, even granting the trend, it is too nebulous to worry about – that, after all, the worthwhile, practical things go on getting themselves done – then this lecture has failed in its purpose. For it has been to show that while there is a whole host of public opinions which can be created by interests, groups, or even individuals, and that these 'public opinions' can bring all kinds of things to pass, it is only the imperceptible, indefinable formation of a climate of feeling that really matters.

I do not ask you to accept this from me alone. I will ask you to listen to one of the wisest and greatest men in all history. A hundred years ago this year, on 21 August 1858, at Ottawa, Illinois, Abraham Lincoln opened his series of debates with Stephen Douglas. On that day Lincoln said:

In this and like communities, public sentiment is everything. With public sentiment, nothing can fail; without it nothing can succeed. Consequently he who moulds public sentiment goes deeper than he who enacts statutes or pronounces decisions. He makes statutes and decisions possible or impossible to be executed.

The most vital task facing us is to make education catch up with politics. By politics I mean every activity of society, 'the body politic' and for a definition of education I go to one of Haldane's favourite quotations: Goethe's saying that 'The object of education ought to be to form tastes rather than simply to communicate knowledge.' The challenge to the free world to-day is not so much a challenge to what we are as to what we can will ourselves to be. We can rejoice that with freedom and full adult suffrage the greatest happiness of the greatest number is at last the guiding principle in affairs. But we shall not survive unless the greatest number have the right values by which to judge wherein true happiness lies.

---

finishing time

163

QUESTIONS

1 British political wisdom (a) is largely a matter of compromise; (b) is based on respect for tradition; (c) can be attributed to the common sense of the leaders; (d) has established an unoppressive authority ( )

2 The author considers that all our freedoms (a) are meaningless unless lower freedoms are sacrificed to higher freedoms; (b) should be inviolate; (c) would constitute a threat to freedom itself if they were not qualified in the light of particular situations; (d) must be subordinated to values such as love and justice if they are to be effective in shaping the future. ( )

3 In his reference to the Press, the author supports the view that (a) newspapers must live for disclosure; (b) today newspapers present all too many facts which might be misunderstood; (c) newspapers should concentrate on information and not express strong views; (d) when presenting information, particularly in national emergencies, newspapers should not reveal information which might lead to confusion. ( )

4 Public bodies and national institutions should (a) present accomplished facts only; (b) oblige their officials to stay silent when their own cause is at stake; (c) not detach themselves from Public Opinion; (d) on all major issues, leave Public Opinion to the politicians. ( )

5 Speaking of the Radio and Press, the author says that the suppression of uncomfortable opinion is (a) wrongly attributed to the demand of the public at large, whose instinct for suppression is grossly exaggerated; (b) the work of the ruling few; (c) usually demanded by the interested parties; (d) a public instinct that is too often under-estimated. ( )

6 The pressure to enforce the orthodox (a) is legitimate only when people are members of organiza-

tions, such as a political party or a trade union; (b) should not alarm us if we believe in liberty through majority rule; (c) amounts to victimization; (d) is no more extreme than the uninhibited expression of opinion.   ( )

7   The stifling of Public Opinion (a) though less extreme than it used to be, causes violent reaction because we have become more conscious of our rights; (b) though dangerous, shows that in practice there can be no unrestricted right to influence people; (c) is the modern way of defending privilege; (d) seems to be met with growing apathy and acquiescence.   ( )

8   The object of education ought to be (a) to form tastes rather than simply to communicate knowledge; (b) to communicate knowledge rather than simply to form tastes; (c) true happiness, here and now; (d) a profound regard for judgement based on accurate information uninfluenced by Public Opinion.   ( )

9   The author's final purpose is to show that (a) it is only the imperceptible, indefinable formation of a climate of feeling that really matters; (b) Public Opinion is less powerful, and less important socially, than public opinions created by interests, groups, or even individuals; (c) fortunately, the control of Public Opinion is not as harmful to society as it might seem to be; (d) Public Opinion is a nebulous sentiment unless it is transformed into public opinions with definite aims.   ( )

10 What are the four freedoms mentioned by the author?

---

speed.........w.p.m. (page 241) comprehension.........(page 235)

Comments

The key to this passage is its uncompromising tone. We must ask ourselves if the four freedoms are inviolate: the assumption is that they should be; but each one of them is being slowly and subtly threatened. From this clean-cut approach it is possible to anticipate the author's attitude to the issues he raises.

Suggestions for Practice

1. Examine any inaccurate answers you may have given to the multiple-choice questions in previous exercises, seeing how far you were influenced by what you thought the author should have said; and make a similar examination of your answers to questions in subsequent exercises. (If, for example, you disagree strongly, as indeed you might, with Professor Young's attitude to the mind [Exercise 9, page 84], you may have misinterpreted 'It is much easier to say that we act as we do because of some entity like the will or super-ego, or something like that,' and your answer to question 7 [page 90] may have been (b) or (c) instead of (a).)

2. Particularly good practice material both for flexible reading and the examination of one's attitudes can be found in Parliamentary Debates (daily Hansard, H.M.S.O., price 1s. 6d.); November, December, and January issues are best, as by then the second readings of major Government bills are under debate. Read the opening and closing speeches, taking each speech as a separate exercise; summarize the main points and check your comprehension and attitudes. Read the debate itself and summarize some of the contributions, again checking your comprehension and attitudes. As so many different views are expressed on the same theme, there is also plenty of scope for anticipation.

CHAPTER 10

MEMORY

EVERYTHING we have said about reading as a digestive process applies to memory. We shall therefore present this chapter in the form of extended notes that will serve as a general summary. (A comparison should be made with Chapter 5.)

General Principles

1. *There is no single, general faculty of memory.* One cannot speak of having a good memory as one can of having good eyesight.

2. *Memory consists of three activities: learning, retaining, and recalling* – assimilating information, retaining it once it has been assimilated, and being able to recollect it at will.

3. *Memory depends on learning*, because no ways have yet been devised for improving retention and recall as separate activities. This explains the connexion between reading, learning, and memory.

4. *There is not one general memory, there are many specialized memories.* The reader who is good at remembering some things may be bad at remembering others, the reason being that specialized interests produce specialized digestive systems. The reader who seems to have a good general memory has wide interests.

5. *There can be no general training in memory.* Improvement cannot be effected by methods such as learning by heart, which treat memory as a single, unspecialized faculty that can be trained for any and every purpose. Training in *one* field may bring improvement, but the skill can only be maintained by constant practice and cannot usually be transferred to other fields.

The Requirements of Good Memory

1. *A motive and an interest.* If the reader allows himself to be coerced by the print, which can easily happen because of the technical problem of communication, then his reading may lack purpose and will certainly lack drive.

The absence of interest in a particular subject usually implies an inadequate digestive system and the reader may have 'no memory' for that subject.

2. *An intention to remember.* This gives the reader a mental 'set', which excludes distractions. Over-concentration, however, may lead to memorizing and the paralysing fear of forgetting.

The reader cannot postpone his intention to remember; but he should not pause at every obstacle, because the meaning may be clarified by the general trend of the argument.

3. *Using one's existing knowledge (anticipation).*

4. *The appropriate method of learning.* There are only two methods of learning: memorizing and understanding. Memorizing, which is a repetitive process, is the only way of remembering completely unrelated items; in reading, memory depends primarily on *learning by understanding*. This involves:

(a) *Selection and organization (the formation of schemas).* The schemas take shape by a process of forgetting the inessentials. (Memorizing, on the other hand, is inclusive, not selective: the aim is to learn by repeating everything and forgetting nothing.)

(b) *Constructive repetition.* This will be considered in Chapter 11 ('Reading Books').

(c) *Stages and intermediate targets.* The reader who does not break the task down into stages (by previewing, etc.) and provide himself with targets may be overpowered by the sight of an unending succession of words: he may therefore over-concentrate through fear of forgetting and resort to memorizing.

The importance of stages and targets will also be considered in Chapter 11 ('Reading Books').

5. *Adequate time.* There must be time for digestion. Time in itself is neutral. The passage of time does not seem to be a cause of forgetting, because whatever is comprehended late at

night seems to lose nothing by the interval of sleep, even if the subject is one the reader easily forgets. Time for digestion is provided by flexibility in reading speed and by a strategy of reading.

6. *The proper distribution of effort.* This again is a matter of flexibility and strategy. The economical distribution of both time and effort requires flexibility because the rate of assimilation cannot be increased. The strategic distribution of effort is particularly important in *long-term memory*. As the reader has innumerable specialized memories, there are likely to be subjects he easily forgets. In such cases forgetting does not usually proceed at a steady, uniform rate; most of the forgetting occurs soon after reading, within the first few weeks or even days, sometimes hours, after which the loss is more gradual. If the reader delays too long before picking up the threads, he may find that very few threads remain and may have as much work on his hands as if he had read nothing at all. His best course is to revise fairly frequently during the first few days by means of skimming and selective reading, and then less frequently, increasing the intervals. In this way he is able to retain most of the information with relatively little effort.

7. *Over-learning.* If knowledge is to be retained with any degree of permanency, there must be over-learning: learning beyond what is necessary for retention in the short term. Readers give more thought than perhaps they realize to things they find interesting, and this is why they remember them so much better; there is a continuing and spontaneous process of learning, for when they reflect on what they have read, and particularly when they discuss it, learning begins all over again and the schemas are worked into new relationships. The most ordinary act of turning a piece of writing over in the mind is not merely a reinforcement of learning, it is an extension of learning, over-learning, a better kind of learning altogether. If reading is to be retained for any length of time, it should be the object of reflection and discussion.

The essence of over-learning is *questioning*. The reader remembers best what he questions most. The questions should be those that raise problems, because people cannot resist the challenge of problems in which they become personally involved and which offer possibilities of solution – even Chinese puzzles. The reader works at unsolved problems, consciously and unconsciously; and what he works at he retains. Furthermore, the continual exploration of the 'whole' mind in search of solutions makes thinking more imaginative, because the transfer of ideas from one department of thought to another gives the reader perspective.

A Note on Note-taking

Note-taking is, of course, an aid to memory, but we are concerned here with some of the dangers of note-taking, the most insidious being the habit of postponing learning by understanding. There are readers who find it difficult to comprehend thoughtful writing without first taking notes; and it is significant that among these are people who in their professional capacity summarize documents and from the summaries draft reports.

Obsessive note-taking is the occupational hazard of students. They believe they remember things best by writing them down. Writing things down, however, is a practice that can be abused: it can so easily lead to a passive and unconfident attitude to books; every little point the student reads may in its context be so persuasive and compelling that he feels constrained to include it in his notes, which become an abridged version of the original. The obsessive note-taker usually postpones learning by understanding till he comes to read his notes; but as these are not always the product of understanding they may be lengthy and unreliable. Furthermore, sentence-by-sentence or paragraph-by-paragraph note-taking commits the reader to page-by-page reading; and as we shall see in the next chapter, this is not necessarily the best way of reading and understanding a book.

The reader's notes should be the outcome of understanding and not the prelude to it. Notes of this kind are brief.

What to Do Next

Previewing

Exercise 16, 'Spartan Training': 10 seconds.

Exercise 17, 'Learning – an Irrational Process': 15 seconds.
(*Previewing is part of your reading time.*)

Anticipation (Exercise 17 only)

When you have finished previewing, do not start reading, but anticipate for a few minutes. *Do* NOT *count this as part of your reading time.*

Reviewing (Exercise 17 only)

As soon as you have finished reading, skim over the passage to refresh your memory. *Count this as part of your reading time.*

(Reviewing is very important. We do not, however, recommend it as a regular training procedure for short passages, because some readers have a habit of reading thoughtful material twice, delaying the effort to comprehend.)

Comprehension

Exercise 16: ten free-answer questions.

Exercise 17: ten multiple-choice questions.

Exercise 16   (1370 words)

SPARTAN TRAINING

Extract from Ancient Education and Today* by E. B. Castle

---

starting time

In his life of Lycurgus Plutarch strikes the keynote of the Spartan system when he explains that the founder of the Lacedaemonian regime 'bred up his citizens in such a way that they neither would nor could live by themselves; they were to make themselves one with the public good and, clustering like bees

* © E. B. Castle, 1961. Pelican Books. Reproduced by permission of the author.

around their commander, be by their zeal and public spirit carried all but out of themselves and devoted wholly to their country'. The long process of conditioning to this subjection began at birth, for in the Lycurgean system the young were deemed much less the children of their parents than the wards of the commonwealth. Each newly born child was displayed before experienced judges of infantile physical fitness, a kind of state health committee, and if 'puny or ill-shaped' was condemned to exposure in the Apothetes, a gorge in the Taygetus mountains. Those surviving the test were preserved for a somewhat less rigorous type of exposure during the rest of their lives, for if the Spartans rid themselves of their worst specimens of childhood they took good care over the rest. Spartan mothers had no use for swaddling bands but exposed the limbs of children to the sun and air. We may assume that there was little gentleness in the early years, and that the austerities that were to descend upon the child of seven were probably applied progressively up to that age. At seven the state took charge and the state training or *agogè* began, covering a period of thirteen years; but in effect this service was a life-sentence.

From seven to eleven the youngest boys lived at home and attended classes for games and physical training; from twelve to fifteen they were snatched from their homes for good to endure rougher treatment in the Spartan boarding school, a juvenile barracks where life was brutal and less than frugal; then followed four years military training. The younger boys were organized into packs and companies, on the lines of our scout patrol and scout group. The pluckiest boy in the pack was appointed leader whose duty it was to lead and punish. Over the packs ruled the Eiren, a young man who had completed his youth training and now took charge of the younger boys. The Eiren was supervised by the Paidonomos, 'one of the best and honestest men in the city' according to Plutarch, with unlimited powers of punishment for slackness and indiscipline, usually administered by his young attendants the 'floggers'. Within this little hierarchy absolute obedience was required by immediate superiors, but beyond its limits every Spartan boy had to obey any adult he might meet in the street. His first and last duty was to obey, and the whip was the first and last sanction for those who had ideas of their own.

From the age of twelve Spartan boys were not allowed to wear an undergarment even in the rigorous Peloponnesian winter; they ate their coarse and scanty rations in common and slept together in rough communal quarters on rushes plucked from the banks of the Eurotas, 'which they break off with their hands without a knife'. A plunge into the river served for a bath. We may readily accept Plutarch's comment that 'their bodies were hard and dry, with but little acquaintance of baths and unguents'; and also his judgement that 'the whole course of their education was one continued exercise of a ready and perfect obedience'.

Rations were kept short in order to stimulate the novice in the art of stealing, an accomplishment it was one of the duties of the Eiren to foster. This young instructor combined the offices of public-school house-master and prefect by organizing a fagging system which supplied his own larder, supplemented the meagre diet of his charges, and at the same time developed the skill in foraging and scout-craft essential to successful soldiering. The boys stole vegetables from their neighbours' fields, meat from the communal kitchen, and fuel from the woods. Such marauding expeditions were not regarded as anti-social behaviour; they were exercises in a specific skill carried out under a strict code of rules. Even the altar of the tribal goddess was brought into useful service for this particular educational purpose. Xenophon observes that the instructors made it a point of honour among the boys 'to steal as many cheeses as possible from the altar of Artemis Orthia, but appointed others to scourge the thieves, meaning to show thereby that by enduring pain for a short time one may win lasting fame and felicity'. Although finesse in theft was a highly regarded accomplishment, it was a disgrace to be found out. For this offence 'they were whipped without mercy for thieving so ill and awkwardly'.

As a further encouragement to toughness the older men urged on the boys to fight each other so that they might learn to endure pugilistic punishment with calm. To flinch under physical assault was a dishonour of high degree. The foraging expeditions of the under-eighteens were but a preparatory course of training for a vicious practice which severely confines our respect to the more acceptable modes of Spartan education: between the ages of eighteen and twenty the young men were organized into a secret service for spying on and liquidating by furtive assassination any Helots suspected of restlessness or rebellion. Thus the final initiation into full citizen status extended training in juvenile theft into murder for political purposes.

We must also note that in effect the whole of Sparta was an armed camp, organized on a basis of fifty-three years military service. Consequently every man under sixty with whom a Spartan child held converse was a soldier trained in a tradition where the ideas of the barrack-room determined the climate of opinion. Throughout their formative years boys and girls were submitted to two major influences – emotionally, to the martial traditions of their race, physically, at least as far as the boys were concerned, to frequent chastisement. Flogging was the unwavering response even to slight offences and minor failures. No other type of direct admonition except the taunts of their elders or the scorn of Spartan maidens seems to have entered into the Spartan boy's upbringing. Complaints or tale-bearing to parents were followed by a repetition of the flogging, because hardness, not justice, was the point at issue: 'If a boy tells his own father when he has been whipped by another father it is a disgrace if the parent does not give his son another whipping.'

Spartan training was, then, concentrated almost exclusively on physical and pre-military fitness. Plutarch admits that some concession is made to literacy: 'Reading and writing they gave them, just enough to serve their turn; their chief care was to make good subjects and to teach them to endure pain and conquer in battle.' Military drill, hunting, swimming, riding, scoutcraft, spying, and strenuous work under supervision in the gymnasium were the sum of the young Spartan's direct education. Handmaidens to this practical teaching were the national songs, the poems of Tyrtaeus, music, and dancing, which were regarded as important instruments for generating the martial spirit. As arithmetic smacked of commerce in which no Spartan engaged, the mysteries of number remained almost unexplored, except in so far as counting of heads was necessary to an army.

While rhetoric was scorned and its teaching forbidden the Spartans respected that shrewdness of mind expressed in the brief and pointed phrase – laconism – for which their speech was renowned, surely immortalized in Leonidas' order of the day at Thermopylae: 'Breakfast here; supper in Hades.' In their dining clubs after supper the elders gave the boys exercise in 'just and sententious answers' to questions of a solidly practical nature aimed at evoking quick juvenile judgement on current affairs. There was nothing on these occasions resembling the Socratic dialogue. In this way, says Plutarch, they informed themselves 'of the abilities and defects of their countrymen' and learned to express their views with brevity and in the style of grim humour in which their elders especially delighted. Any youth who failed to satisfy the standards of his elders had his thumb bitten by the master.

---

finishing time

QUESTIONS

1 According to Plutarch what was the keynote of the Spartan system?

2 What happened to all newly born children?

3 What training did boys undergo (a) from twelve to fifteen? (b) for the next four years?

4 What was the first and last duty of a Spartan boy?

5 (a) Why were the boy's rations kept in short supply? (b) For what offence were they whipped without mercy?

6 What was the training for final initiation into full citizen status?

7 What was the whole purpose of Spartan training?

8 What part did reading, writing, and arithmetic play in Spartan training?

9 Why were young Spartans taught the national songs, the poems of Tyrtaeus, music, and dancing?

10 What was the main purpose of the exercises given to boys by their elders after supper?

---

speed.........w.p.m. (page 242) comprehension.........(page 238)

Comments

If you are familiar with the subject it will be interesting to note how this has affected your speed; even expert knowledge does not influence speed as much as one might expect.

Exercise 17 (920 words)

LEARNING – AN IRRATIONAL PROCESS

Extract from *The Science of Behaviour** by John McLeish

Preview for 15 seconds; then anticipate

---

starting time

Because knowing belongs to the realm of the rational most people tend to take too intellectualistic a view of learning. That the act of learning is based on irrational processes is over-looked. Because of a widespread, but mistaken belief that education is nothing more than the provision of 'facts' to be stored, the learner is thought of as an 'empty vessel, waiting to be filled' (Thomas Carlyle). The teaching function is conceived solely in terms of imparting information. The teacher is a doler out of 'facts' in quantities appropriate to the 'capacity' of the pupil. Learning is equated with the outcome 'knowing' which appertains to our rational nature.

It is certainly true that an essential and important part of the educator's task is the imparting of relevant information. But examine what remains from our school and university days and we find not a collection of discrete facts, but rather an

* Reproduced by permission of Pemberton Publishing Co. in conjunction with Barrie and Rockliff.

attitude to life. Only those who will become teachers need concern themselves with hoarding 'facts' as the squirrel hoards nuts.

Most of those who have written about education distinguish between *education* and *instruction.* To mention only one example: Herbart says that 'Instruction forms the circle of thought: education the character. The last is nothing without the first. Herein is contained the whole sum of my pedagogical doctrine.' To complete Herbart's thought we must add that the first (instruction and the circle of thought) is nothing without the last (education and character). Instruction is not the same as education. It is one of the instruments by means of which people *become* educated. Herbart says in another place: 'The one task and the whole task of education may be summed up in the concept of morality.'

In transmitting what has been miscalled the 'hard fact' the educator is also transmitting, unawares and willy-nilly, an *attitude* to facts and to life. It is almost invariably forgotten by the educator that it is the *attitude* which remains after the 'hard facts' have disappeared into the limbo of the forgotten.

These assertions are clarified when we recognize that education (like experience in general) involves a process of *selection* in which the data are in some measure *created* by the educator and *re-created* by the person being educated. Culture is never transmitted unaltered. The transmitter and the recipient both significantly modify the cultural heritage in the educational moment. It is one of the conditions of progress. In primitive (that means unprogressive) societies there are no critics: culture is an absolute or dogma which is passed on without any alteration or selection.

The implication of all this is that there can be no such thing as *objectivity in teaching* if by this is meant a passionless, disinterested search for neutral data by an unprejudiced group under the direction of an unemotional teacher. Human beings never were and probably never will be constituted in this way. This view of objectivity and education implies that the educator and the person being educated are completely structureless, with external reality a kind of administrator's dream with every-

177

thing classified and ticketed, each element existing in a clearly defined, watertight compartment. But education implies organization or structure not only in the *material* but in the *persons* involved. Its successful outcome involves a limitation of what Goethe calls 'the omnipotence of the random will'. In chess, for example, one learns to do quite extraordinary things within the limits imposed by the game. But this means that the infinite variety of response of the totally uninstructed person is no longer possible. Learning involves specialization and specialization implies selection and a limitation of response.

Sir John Adams has said that 'the knowledge that counts, the knowledge that is power, is not mere acquaintance with fact. It is experience of facts in their relation to each other.' This actually is how the process of selection operates. Facts are chosen to exhibit relationships: these relationships are decided upon on the basis of their place in a hierarchy of importance by the educator. The process of ordering the facts and their presentation in terms of hierarchies of importance are largely unconscious. Few teachers persistently ask themselves the question: Why am I trying to teach this particular content just at this particular time? Is A as important as X, Y, Z in terms of what people should know? What do I mean by 'important'?

It is clear that there is a very strong element of irrationality in the selection of the 'facts' which the teacher wishes to transmit. Equally there are numerous irrational factors which operate in the process of transmission, making this process possible. They operate outside of the awareness either of the educator or of the person being educated. These irrational processes invariably give 'colour' to the 'facts', they make the 'facts' interesting in such a way that without them no educational process would be possible.

---

finishing time

QUESTIONS

1 What most people tend to overlook is that (a) capacity varies from individual to individual; (b)

learning is based on irrational processes; (c) learning is a rational process; (d) learning is only concerned with imparting relevant information. ( )

2 What remains from our school and university days is (a) a collection of facts; (b) prejudices and uncritical attitudes; (c) an attitude to life; (d) the ability to reason. ( )

3 According to the author (a) there is no difference between good education and good instruction; (b) what we need is education, not instruction; (c) we need more instruction and less so-called education; (d) instruction is one of the means by which we become educated. ( )

4 'Hard facts' (a) are what remain when attitudes have been forgotten; (b) save us from prejudice; (c) can only be transmitted with an attitude to facts and to life; (d) are facts that are beyond dispute. ( )

5 Education involves (a) a process of selection; (b) the acceptance of traditional values; (c) a corporate spirit; (d) respect for authority. ( )

6 The author's view is that a passionless, disinterested search for neutral data (a) cannot exist; (b) is true objectivity; (c) is only possible for those who are free from prejudice; (d) is only possible when a clear distinction is made between reason and emotion. ( )

7 Education implies organization or structure (a) in society; (b) in teaching establishments; (c) in the methods of instruction; (d) in the material and in the persons involved. ( )

8 The outcome of successful learning is (a) unlimited specialization; (b) less specialization; (c) a limitation of response; (d) an infinite variety of response. ( )

9 The process of ordering the facts and their presentation in hierarchies of importance (a) is largely unconscious; (b) must be made fully conscious; (c) brings us nearer to ultimate Truth; (d) depends merely on acquaintance with fact. ( )

10 No educational process would be possible without

(a) emphasis on reason; (b) a clear distinction between facts and values; (c) a very strong element of
irrationality; (d) emphasis on values.   (   )

---

speed.........w.p.m. (page 241) comprehension.........(page 235)

Comments

This passage expresses ideas that are reflected in much of the
text of this book and in many of the reading exercises. You will
certainly have recalled some of the related ideas while anticipating; and others will have occurred to you while summarizing, if you have done this before answering the questions. The
ability to relate ideas in this way is the outcome of reading that
is characterized by quick anticipation, sensitivity to tone, and a
high level of inner questioning – activities that make further
reading easier and far more imaginative, retentive, and
enjoyable.

As an exercise, read through the passage again, and as you do
so make a list of the most striking words and phrases. Against
them write related ideas that have occurred in the previous
texts, notes, and reading exercises; do this from memory, referring back to chapter headings, subheadings, and the titles of
exercises. Below we give a few suggestions, a list that is by no
means exhaustive. Check your list against ours, which follows
these comments, and compare the results with what actually
came to mind while you were anticipating (and summarizing).

(The reader does not normally reflect on a multitude of
related ideas while he is reading; they are there in his understanding, as an *attitude* to the facts. When he anticipates, either
before reading or while he is reading, a few intimations can
activate the whole of his mind, and one or two subsequent questions help to organize his ideas into a related body of knowledge.)

RELATED IDEAS – EXERCISE 17

Irrational process: Ch. 9, 'Attitudes'.

Facts to be stored: Ch. 3, 'Reading'; Ch. 10, 'Memory'; Ex. 11, 'Universal Histories'.

Empty vessel: Ch. 3, 'Reading'; Ch. 6, 'Skimming'.

Attitude to life: Ch. 9, 'Attitudes'; Ex. 9, 'Seeing and Believing' (we see what we believe); Ex. 10, 'Art and Artists' (no wrong reason for liking pictures); Ex. 11, 'Universal Histories' (personal nature of selection); Ex. 15, 'Public Opinion' (education to form tastes rather than to communicate knowledge).

Instruction and education: Ex. 11, 'Universal Histories'; Ex. 12, 'Bell Telephone's Experiment' (educated rather than well-trained men).

Circle of thought: Introduction; Introduction to Part II (diagram); Ch. 3, 'Reading'; Ex. 5, 'Look at a Threepenny Piece' (whole thought).

Selection: Ch. 3, 'Reading'; Ch. 9, 'Attitudes'; Ch. 10, 'Memory'; Ex. 9, 'Seeing and Believing' (selection of familiar patterns); Ex. 11, 'Universal Histories' (wholesale selection and truthful selection).

Created and re-created: Introduction; Introduction to Part II; Ex. 5, 'Look at a Threepenny Piece'.

Dogma: Ex. 3, 'Tears' (our fashions are right and proper); Ex. 10, 'Art and Artists' (preconceived ideas); Ex. 11, 'Universal Histories' (correct opinions); Ex. 15, 'Public Opinion' (the Party line; pressure to enforce the orthodox).

Objectivity and neutral data: Ch. 2, 'Note on Comprehension Tests'; Ch. 9, 'Attitudes' (quotation from Darwin); Ex. 9, 'Seeing and Believing' (interpret in terms of our own world); Ex. 10, 'Art and Artists' (standards vary); Ex. 11, 'Universal Histories' (groping towards order and coherence); Ex. 12, 'Bell Telephone's Experiment' (no one solution to many problems).

Administrator's dream: Ex. 1, 'Ends and Means' (administrator's fallacy: looking upon society as a systematic whole).

Watertight compartments: Ch. 7, 'Anticipation'; Ch. 10, 'Memory'; Ex. 11, 'Universal Histories'.

Organization and structure: Ch. 3, 'Reading'; Ch. 9, 'Attitudes';
   Ch. 10, 'Memory'; Ex. 9, 'Seeing and Believing' (framework).
Relationships: Ch. 3, 'Reading'; Ch. 6, 'Skimming'; etc.
Irrational processes in transmission: Ex. 4, 'Trouble with
   People' (behaviour makes sense in terms of goals, needs and
   motives); Ex. 15, 'Public Opinion' (climate of feeling).
Colour: Ch. 3, 'Note on Digests'; Ch. 9, 'Attitudes'.

Suggestions for Practice

Refer to the next chapter, which outlines a method of reading
books.

CHAPTER 11

READING BOOKS

THE skills of perspective – skimming, anticipation, and organization – culminate in the reading of *informative* books. You should now begin to practise on books. Start with something that interests you, a book perhaps you have been waiting to read; not necessarily an easy book, but one that has not too many sectional topics; a book with a theme.

The Method of Phased Reading

What we now describe is more than an exercise, it is a *method*. We do not advocate procedures, however, and the following is meant to suggest the method, not to prescribe a set of rules. On the face of it the explanation may seem involved, but the purpose is clear: to reconstruct the author's thought. Something like this:

(a) Read the blurb and inspect the contents page. Read the preface and introduction (leave the introduction at this stage if it is virtually the first chapter). Examine the index, which may show the relative importance of the areas of thought and provide a pattern of concepts; this stimulates anticipation and facilitates skimming.

(b) Preview the first and last chapters by sampling the first and last paragraphs or thereabouts and the first few lines of the other paragraphs. There should be nothing rigid about this and you should always be on the alert for synopses, summaries, headings, italics, and typographical aids. If the book is in parts, you may have to preview each part.

Ten minutes are usually enough for (a) and (b).

(c) Spend a little time anticipating the contents and asking questions.

(d) Preview the other chapters, skimming more freely.

Allow about ten minutes for this.

183

(e) Anticipate; ask questions.

(f) Read the main text straight through for a *general* understanding, skimming and skipping where necessary and reading selectively. Mark important passages (a vertical stroke in the margin is a good way) and difficult parts that need to be read again (a double line perhaps); or make a note of the pages (which is useful in any case).

(g) Study the difficult passages, taking as long as you need.

(h) Make a mental summary of the general theme of the book.

(i) You may now wish to re-read the book for a more detailed knowledge of the contents. Only stages (a) to (h) are required for the exercise.

The method we have recommended, which we call phased reading, is so important that we now propose to consider its advantages.

Phased Reading and the Laws of Learning

In the first place, it accords fully with the 'laws' of learning. The reader has perspective: he can therefore anticipate, ask questions, and use his existing knowledge. The schemas evolve organically: the mind has time to assimilate, and with each phase there is a constructive repetition – over-learning – which makes retention easier. And there are intermediate goals, so that the reader is not overwhelmed by the task.

Secondly, it is satisfying. This phased operation might seem like cold-blooded dissection, but it is not so: if the book (we are not speaking of novels) is finely written, it loses nothing of its aesthetic surprise by being read in this way. We can see no advantage in the straight-through method, except that by taking longer to achieve less it can be pleasantly relaxing; and if this is the reader's unmistakable purpose there is nothing to be said against it. But it is distressing to see a student misapplying his effort and wasting time, unconsciously trying to memorize one book as though it were a Bible, when what he needs is the excitement and stimulation of many.

Thirdly, it is purposeful, because the reader can carry his

reading to the requisite *level* of comprehension; whereas if he follows the line of print and then abandons the project, he may achieve nothing.

And lastly, there is a genuine *relationship* between author and reader. Ideally an author should write in different ways for different groups of readers according to their interests and knowledge (just as the teacher adapts his presentation to the personality of his class); but as this is impossible, he must address himself to his average reader and cannot, therefore, expect everyone to hang on every word he utters. It seems to us that a *degree* of understanding is better for author and reader alike than a tiresome relationship or even the broken one of a book half finished. Moreover, time is of the essence of reading and however worthy a book may be, there are other authors to consider. Many books, of course, require a full and complete understanding; and to some the reader will return again and again – the relationship becomes permanent.

In conclusion, phased reading needs less effort and takes less time than the straight-through method *for what it achieves*: knowledge that can be retained and used; but it is the antithesis of lazy reading.

PART III

*

ADDITIONAL EXERCISES

CHAPTER 12

WHAT TO DO NEXT

IN order to prepare you for the final test, we have provided four straightforward passages with comprehension questions; these you will read without comment from us. *Preview each passage for 10 seconds.*

As a reminder that efficient reading requires strategy, and is as much concerned with saving time and effort as with the ability to read at speed, we have included a long, complex exercise ('The Hawthorne Investigations') with twenty free-answer questions; for this we shall suggest a method of reading.

Suggestions for Practice

1. You should read at least one book in the way we have suggested. The method we outlined in the last chapter is only intended as a guide; so do not adopt any rigid procedure.

2. In addition, try some long passages that offer scope for flexible reading. As part of the exercise, practise anticipating, previewing, and reviewing; test your comprehension by means of summaries; and use the summaries to analyse your methods of reading.

3. If you are still rather slow, you should preview more extensively, so that when you come to read you have the framework of the article in mind: this helps you to anticipate, think for yourself while you are reading, use your existing knowledge more fully, and leap forward from one vantage point to another over ground that is not completely unfamiliar.

4. Looking for the right kind of practice material is in itself excellent practice in previewing and skimming.

Exercise 18 (1370 words)

THE TASTES AND FASHIONS OF THE ROMANTICS

Extract from *Taste and Fashion** by James Laver

starting time

The Romanticist looked back to former ages, and if he did so with such passion it was largely because he was dissatisfied with his own. Even when the desire to reach back in history had faded the *malaise* remained. We may laugh, in retrospect, at the *maladie d'un enfant du siècle*, but it was a malady which was universal. Byron regarded himself as a blighted being; but so did almost every other young man of sensibility in the early thirties. It is even more curious that women did so too. It was as if, after the orgies of the post-Revolutionary period, everyone in the world had awakened with a headache. Frank paganism and robust health seemed to have vanished together. It is startling to note the number of girls who 'went into a decline' and died before they had reached womanhood. Some have suggested that the extraordinary prevalence of consumption during the Restoration period was due to the very inadequate clothing of the previous generation; but in the face of modern medical opinion it is hard to believe that anybody was ever much worse for wearing little. No, the invalidism of the Romantics was largely a matter of mentality. It was none the less frequently mortal, and this is perhaps the most astonishing thing about it.

Tight-lacing may be considered either as a cause or merely as a symptom of the prevailing tendency. Women began to suffer from perpetual migraine, to look pale and faint upon sofas at the slightest provocation. To be fat was almost a crime, and even to look healthy was something approaching a solecism. An ideal fragility was the prevailing mode, and to attain it women were willing to suffer martyrdom. To eat heartily was a mark of grossness, and to such an extreme was this idea carried that many women found it necessary to make a meal at home before going out to dine. It will be remembered that

* Reproduced by permission of the author and George G. Harrap & Co.

Byron at one time confined himself to a diet of potatoes sprinkled with vinegar. 'How long will his lordship persist in his present diet?' asked one of his friends. 'Just as long as you continue to notice it,' returned another; and there was no doubt an element of ostentation in all such privations. Yet there were some – far too many – who took their vinegar-drinking in earnest. Schoolgirls in convents drank it in order to have a look of illness, to keep thin; they sat up all night reading to give themselves heavy eyes with black rings underneath them. Among fashionable ladies there was an enormous consumption of belladonna, a drug which dilated the pupils of the eyes and gave them a wild, fixed appearance. There was a rage for the Spanish type, black-haired and green as a lemon. So sallow was the prevailing complexion in 1835 that a memoirist of the period compares the contemporary beauties with the Chinese and Japanese. Some, both men and women, even made up with yellow pigment. Men strove to look pale and distinguished, as if ravaged by some secret sorrow; women to look frail and afflicted with a settled melancholy. It was as if universal lunacy had settled upon the fashionable world. The Byronic hero, with his cadaverous features and sarcastic smile, was to be seen everywhere, flanked by women with faces like alabaster, almost transparent, just rescued from the tomb and liable at any moment to return to it.

Barbey d'Aurevilly called Byron the 'solar plexus' of the nineteenth century, and in the early thirties it seemed to be no less than the truth. Almost all the principal Romantic writers were dark men with pale complexions. An element of fatalism seemed to be necessary to any kind of popular success. In all the pictures of the day we can see them with their morose expression and their high foreheads, sometimes made higher still by the plucking out of the hairs. So extraordinary can be the influence of one man of genius when his temper is mysteriously in tune with the spirit of the age.

The evolution of men's costume during the Romantic period was largely similar to that of women. Men too were influenced by the vogue of fancy-dress balls, and some of them even wore medieval costumes in the street. Some wore pointed medieval shoes and strove to make their waistcoats look like doublets. The famous *gilet rouge* of Théophile Gautier was not a waistcoat at all – it was a doublet; but its influence was all the greater for that fact. Even when waistcoats were waistcoats they were generally red or some red shade, and a violently coloured waistcoat of some kind was *de rigueur*. Any eccentricity was permissible if it enabled men to break away from the *bourgeois* costume of the day. . . .

The main difference, however, between *bourgeois* and Romantic was in the matter of beard. Except for the small sidewhiskers which had come in with the Empire, the majority of men in 1830 were clean-shaven. The beard had scarcely been seen since the early seventeenth century; but now all that was changed. The Romantics made it a point of honour to grow a beard, and it is interesting to note that this was such an outrage on prevailing custom that the first beards were hooted by children in the streets of Paris. Nevertheless the beards won; so that in retrospect the nineteenth century seems to us a bearded century, almost as completely as the eighteenth century is an unbearded one. . . .

It is strange to reflect that it was probably Bulwer-Lytton's influence, reinforced by the Romantic passion for sombre hues, which established, once for all, the black evening coat which has lasted to the present day. Before the Romantic period evening coats had been of various colours, but before the middle of the century it became good form to wear a black one, and this proved so convenient, both to the ladies, who were not likely to have their colour scheme ruined by the coats of their partners, and to the men themselves, to whom the black evening coat was a real economy, that the custom perpetuated itself. Many attempts have been made since to revive coloured coats, but they have met with very limited success. Black evening dress is too useful. It is perhaps the only successful conspiracy of the consumer, who has managed to get his own convenience labelled with the sign of good form. It is a curious result of the alliance of romantic melancholy and fashionable hauteur. . . .

We have spoken already of the ideal fragility of women so much admired in the Romantic period. This was partly rein-

forced by the immense success of a single ballet. *La Sylphide*
was first produced in 1827, when Taglioni danced the rôle in a
dress of white muslin with underskirt of the same material. So
great was her success that she stereotyped ballet costume for
the rest of the century. Her influence on contemporary dress
was no less important, for she inaugurated a rage for white and
flimsy materials – not used, as they had been at the beginning
of the century, in order to define and reveal the figure, but to
wrap woman up, as it were, in a haze of moonlight. She power-
fully reinforced the other-worldly ideal; she provided a starting-point for a sentimental dream, and when the orgies and
excesses of Romanticism were over it was this dream which
persisted and gave its colour to the succeeding age. For it is the
bourgeoisie, the respectable people, who finally decide what a
fashion shall be, although they very rarely inaugurate it. What
they do is to assimilate as much as they can from the intellectual mode of the period and turn it to their own uses. There
was obviously much in Romanticism which could find no place
in any respectable family. The successful lawyer or banker of
the period had no desire to see his daughters turned into
femmes fatales. So in their hands the Romantic impulse became
refined away into a somewhat mawkish sentimentality. It is this,
and its influence on fashion, which we must consider in the
next chapter.

finishing time

QUESTIONS

1 Almost every man of sensibility in the early thirties
   regarded himself as (a) an eccentric; (b) a hero; (c)
   a blighted being; (d) a poet.   (   )

2 The extraordinary prevalence of consumption
   among women was (a) due to a lack of fresh air and
   proper food; (b) the result of the very inadequate
   clothing of the previous generation; (c) a consequence of tight lacing; (d) largely a mental condition. (   )

3 The prevailing mode among women was (a) an ideal

fragility; (b) moral fervour; (c) whimsicality; (d) poetic feeling. ( )

4 Schoolgirls in convents drank vinegar (a) in imitation of Byron's diet of potatoes and vinegar; (b) to remind themselves of martyrdom; (c) to look ill and keep thin; (d) to overcome their pleasure in food. ( )

5 There was a rage for a type of woman described as (a) Spanish; (b) Chinese; (c) slightly lunatic; (d) pink and white like Dresden china. ( )

6 Almost all the principal writers were (a) dreamy, gentle creatures; (b) dark men with pale complexions; (c) sufferers from an ailment of the solar plexus; (d) unmitigated fatalists. ( )

7 The *main* difference in fashion between the Romantics and the *bourgeoisie* was that the Romantics (a) were, like their women, influenced by the vogue of fancy-dress balls; (b) wore violently coloured waistcoats; (c) wore pointed medieval shoes; (d) made it a point of honour to grow a beard. ( )

8 The black evening coat was probably established (a) as a means of economy; (b) by Bulwer-Lytton's influence, reinforced by the Romantic passion for sombre hues; (c) because women did not wish to have their colour scheme ruined by the coats of their partners; (d) because, even before the Romantic period, it was good form to wear black. ( )

9 The effect of *La Sylphide* was to create a fashion in women's clothes that was (a) voluptuous; (b) frivolous; (c) used to define and reveal the figure; (d) a starting-point for a sentimental dream. ( )

10 The reaction of the *bourgeoisie* to Romanticism was (a) to crusade against it; (b) to refine it away into a somewhat mawkish sentimentality; (c) to make it vulgar and pretentious; (d) to emulate its finer points. ( )

speed.........w.p.m. (page 242) comprehension.........(page 235)

Exercise 19 (980 words)

THE ROAD TO SALVATION

Extract from *England in the Eighteenth Century** by J. H. Plumb

---

starting time

Wesley believed profoundly in salvation and rebirth, for that was the deepest experience of his own life, but unlike the Moravians, he did not regard this as the final consummation of a religious life. Unlike Calvinist Whitfield, he did not believe salvation to be pre-ordained. Susannah Wesley had regarded the theological position of both Moravians and Calvinists as deadly dangerous, and she had insisted on Wesley breaking with both even at cost of splitting his own young movement. She saved Methodism as a social force for good works: a relentless, active, selfless Christian life became the Methodist ideal. Thrift, abstinence, hard work, and concentration were the essential virtues of those seeking salvation and those saved. The puritan ideal was reborn shorn of its political radicalism.

As a way of life, there can be no doubt of Methodism's appeal; it contained so much that was capable of satisfying the deepest needs of human nature. In the exercise of religion there was no emotional restraint. Sobbing, weeping, laughter, hysteria were commonplaces of Methodist fervour – a lack of restraint which seems to us almost pathological. But there was an edge to life in the eighteenth century which is hard for us to recapture. In every class there is the same taut neurotic quality – fantastic gambling and drinking, the riots, brutality and violence, and everywhere and always a constant sense of death. At no point did the Anglican or Dissenting churches of the day touch this inner tragedy of man, which was the emotional core of Methodism. But Methodism gave far more than emotional release; it brought a sense of purpose and a field for the exercise of both will and power.

To men and women who were just climbing out of utter

* © J. H. Plumb, 1950, Pelican Books. Reproduced by permission of the author.

poverty by the dint of their own thrifty endeavour this concentration of will and purpose was particularly appealing. The oligarchical and rigid nature of local institutions meant that there was little scope for ambitious men and women with a social conscience. All doors were closed to them, including, of course, those of the established Church, but Wesley provided an organization in which they could fulfil their need for power and their sense of duty.

Unfortunately, Methodism appealed to other, less socially valuable, sides of human nature. There was nothing intellectual about Methodism; the rational attitude, the most fashionable intellectual attitude of the day, was absolutely absent. Wesley believed in witches, in the corporeal existence of the Devil, and in possession by devils. He made decisions by opening his Bible at random and obeying whatever command he might discover from the first words which met his eye. Wesley's superstitions were those of his uneducated audiences. He produced a little book on physic which was on sale at all meeting-houses. It is an absurd, fantastic compilation of uncritical folk-lore. The leaves of the celandine are to be placed under the foot as a cure for jaundice and three pounds of quicksilver swallowed ounce by ounce will untwist a gut. Everywhere in early Methodism one meets the prejudices of the uneducated, which always seem to be hardened by success. There was an anti-intellectual, philistine quality which attracted the dispossessed but was dangerous for society.

It was at its worst in its attitude to education. Wesley considered play unworthy of a Christian child and, except to produce lay preachers to carry on the good work, he was uninterested in teaching. He considered a knowledge of the Bible and of the Catechism sufficient education for any child, and idle minutes he regarded as of the greatest danger to the child's soul. For the sake of its everlasting life it ought to be at work. Wesley more often than not was preaching in districts with an ever-growing demand for child labour. At the beginning of the century there had been a vigorous movement for primary education, which, if supported and strengthened by Methodism, might have survived the increased pressure from industry. But it got no support at all, and education and the children suffered. The successful Methodist could regard his overworked children with a complacent heart.

In any violent religious fervour, intense hate as well as intense love seems a necessary concomitant; Methodism was no exception. It encouraged a violent hatred of Papists and did all it could to maintain the laws against them. Jews were the murderers of Christ. Any criticism which tended to cast doubt on the literal interpretation of the Bible was the work of the Devil. There was a rabid envy of luxury and elegance, of the aristocratic and libertarian attitude to life.

'To speak the rough truth,' Wesley said, 'I do not desire any intercourse with any persons of quality in England.'

Nor did his flock; the spirit was best preserved amid the ugliness of suburbs and industrial villages through discipline and toil.

Although it was a strange quixotic mixture, a reactionary core in the most socially radical class; strengthening those moral virtues which were to transform English society because they were fitted to economic needs and economic opportunities, impelling willy-nilly a society with implicit faith in *laissez-faire* to a closer knit social organization than mankind had ever known before. As Methodism came to judge human virtue by its social value, it lost its own soul in the pure fervour, the flame-like quality it gave to personal salvation. At 84, Wesley wrote:

The Methodists in every place grow diligent and frugal; consequently they increase in goods. Hence they proportionably increase in pride, in anger, in the desire of the flesh, the desire of the eyes, and the pride of life. So, although the form of religion remains, the spirit is swiftly vanishing away.

Few men have written a more dispassionate, or truer, epitaph on their own life work. But for the next five years he went serenely on, preaching, praying, exhorting, and his last words were: 'I'll praise, I'll praise.'

finishing time

QUESTIONS

1 Susannah Wesley (a) believed, with Wesley, that salvation was the final consummation of a religious life; (b) like Wesley, had puritan ideals in every respect; (c) believed salvation to be preordained; (d) saved Methodism as a social force for good works. (   )

2 Methodism owed its appeal to (a) opportunities for emotional release; (b) a sense of purpose and a field for the exercise of will and power; (c) an almost pathological lack of restraint; (d) the release it gave from the fear of death. (   )

3 As a way of life Methodism appealed to men and women who (a) were just climbing out of utter poverty by their own thrift and endeavour; (b) believed passionately in all the socially valuable sides of human nature; (c) were opposed to the established Church; (d) were appalled by the gambling, drinking, riots, brutality, and violence in every class. (   )

4 The rational attitude was (a) swamped by emotionalism; (b) subordinated to faith; (c) allowed as much scope as possible within the limits of current orthodoxy; (d) absolutely absent. (   )

5 Wesley's position with regard to superstition caused him to (a) believe in witches, the corporeal existence of the Devil, and possession by devils; (b) do all he could to maintain the laws against the Papists; (c) ban an absurd, fantastic book of physic which was on sale at all meeting-houses; (d) attack the mad superstitions of the uneducated. (   )

6 Wesley's concern for children led to a conviction that (a) it was natural for them to love play; (b) idle moments were the greatest danger to the soul: children ought to be at work; (c) the ever-growing employment of child labour was an affront to God and man; (d) overworked children had no time to acquire a fruitful knowledge of the Scriptures. (   )

7 Wesley's views on education were the outcome of (a)

an anti-intellectual, philistine quality that was dangerous for society; (b) the need to produce lay preachers to carry on the good work; (c) the vigorous movement for primary education that existed at the beginning of the century; (d) a blinding conviction that knowledge of the Bible and of the Catechism was sufficient education for any child.　　( )

8　Wesley's attitude to 'persons of quality' in England was (a) to maintain that they were predestined to eternal damnation; (b) to go out of his way to bring them salvation; (c) to have no truck with them at all; (d) unlike his flock, to have a sneaking regard for their aristocratic way of life.　　( )

9　Methodism strengthened those moral virtues which were to transform English society because they were (a) fitted to economic needs and economic opportunities; (b) necessary for a close-knit social organization; (c) the outcome of a doctrine of personal salvation; (d) inspired by an implicit faith in *laissez faire*.　　( )

10　Methodists are described by the author as (a) diligent, frugal, and disciplined people who, nevertheless, lacked Wesley's vision; (b) a thrifty, virtuous community in a brutal, libertarian society; (c) sinners who found their souls in the pure fervour of personal salvation; (d) a reactionary core in the most socially radical class.　　( )

---

speed........w.p.m. (pages 241–2) comprehension........(page 235)

The following exercise is a complex passage that requires not only extended previewing, but reviewing. The purpose is a good general understanding without waste of time and effort. If your speed and comprehension score for this passage compare with your standard in Exercises 1 and 2, you have made considerable progress; and you should be able to read the remaining passages with confidence and ease.

The article describes some combined investigations into

working conditions and output in industry. You should therefore concentrate on the movement of the whole: the purpose,
general nature, and results of *each* investigation; and how the
various investigations are related to one another. Keep an eye
on places where you may expect to find preliminary or summarizing statements that bind the parts together. Complex passages
with a 'problem' type of organization usually have headings;
watch for these and for clues to organization.

Previewing

Take 1¼ minutes; longer, if necessary. *Count this as part of
your reading time.* Sample the text; but let yourself be guided
by the presentation.

Reading

When you have finished previewing, do not pause but read
the passage straight through.

Reviewing

When you have finished reading, do not pause but skim over
the passage to clarify your ideas or refresh your memory. *Count
this as part of your reading time.*

Comprehension

There are twenty free-answer questions requiring very short
answers.

Exercise 20   (2560 words)

How a group of working girls started a revolution in industry

THE HAWTHORNE INVESTIGATIONS –
A MORAL CHALLENGE
by Eric De Leeuw

starting time

In 1927, at the Hawthorne Works of the Western Electric Company in Chicago, Elton Mayo began the most far-reaching re-

searches into working conditions and human relationships that have ever been made. They lasted for six years, until 1933. They are particularly relevant to our present situation because of the light they throw on the problems of restriction of output and resistance to change.

THE BACKGROUND TO THE INVESTIGATIONS

In order to grasp the significance of these investigations it is necessary to understand the position at that time. Fundamental attitudes had scarcely changed since the beginning of the industrial era: it was taken for granted that work was unpleasant; that workers were isolated units; that the only incentive was the carrot or the stick; and that, financially, everyone was out for himself. Towards the end of the eighteenth century, Robert Owen had pleaded with his fellow industrialists to treat workers with the care bestowed on machines. 'It pays,' he kept reminding them plaintively. But such ideas, limited as they were, remained the height of idealism for the next hundred years. Then in the United States at the end of the nineteenth century the concept of scientific management sprang from the brow of F. W. Taylor, who gave convincing demonstrations of how workers could operate with the scientific efficiency of machines; so the emphasis changed from the worker as a machine, in the sense of being *nothing more* than a machine, to the worker as a human machine.

In Britain, scientific management started somewhat later, during the First World War, and then under the guise of industrial psychology. Britain was fighting a war of production. Large numbers of women were employed on dangerous work. To increase output, studies were made of selection, training, hours of work, fatigue, rest pauses, heating, lighting, ventilation, movement, layout, and, of course, accidents. Industrial psychology in those days was the study of the human machine in its physical environment: it had nothing whatever to do with individuals working in groups under supervision.

Elton Mayo and the investigators at the Hawthorne Works were obviously men of unusual insight. Nevertheless, like their British counterparts, they accepted the beliefs of their time:

the philosophy of the *human machine*. They assumed there was a simple, direct relation between output and physical conditions. Then something happened which gave them pause. There had been an experiment at the Hawthorne Works to determine the connexion between illumination and output. The results were topsy-turvy. On one occasion when the light bulbs were changed, the workers were allowed to assume that there was more light. Actually there was not: the bulbs were the same as before; yet the workers spoke approvingly of better lighting; and output increased. It occurred to the investigators that human factors might be involved. The stage was set for experiments that have had prodigious consequences for our thinking about industry.

THE HAWTHORNE INVESTIGATIONS

There were three investigations:
1. The Relay Assembly Test-Room (1927–33);
2. The Interviewing Programme (1928–30);
3. The Bank Wiring Observation Room (1931–32).

As they were interrelated, it is necessary to keep them in perspective. Let us first consider the general pattern of development. The main investigation, The Relay Assembly Test-Room, studied the connexion between physical working conditions and production. A record was kept of the output of a small group of girls. When conditions were improved, output went up; when conditions reverted to what they were before, output not only stayed up, but continued to increase. The girls said they could work better because they were not supervised. As a matter of fact, under the investigator who had charge of them, they were subject to much closer supervision and more frequent and trying changes than ever before. The Company realized it knew little about workers as *human beings*. So while this major investigation was still proceeding, a second investigation was undertaken, the vast Interviewing Programme, in order to learn about workers as human beings. The investigators discovered that conscientious workers harboured all manner of imaginary fears and grievances. The Company wanted to know how these attitudes affected work on the shop floor. This led to the third investigation, the observation of an actual working group under normal conditions. It was found that the men, whose level of production compared favourably with that of other workers, were deliberately restricting output and producing below their capacity.

We shall now examine these three investigations more closely; then we shall consider what it is about modern industry, even when management is well-intentioned, that makes responsible and co-operative workers restrict output and resist change. In these investigations it is possible to study the facts dispassionately and objectively because there was no question of Communist infiltration, restrictive practices, shop-steward activities or political attitudes: the workers were go-ahead Americans, and the Company had not had a strike for many years.

1. *The Relay Assembly Test-Room* (*1927–33*). The object was to study the effects on output of changes in physical working conditions. Six average girls, employed in the assembly of telephone relays, agreed to take part in the experiment. The work of assembling relays was such that even the slightest changes in output could be measured. A room was partitioned off in the department. The equipment and the benches were unchanged, except that there was a hole in each bench into which the completed relays were dropped; the relays then passed along a chute so that output could be measured electrically. A log was kept, not only of output and changes in working conditions, but of every change likely to affect the girls, even changes in the weather, the number of hours spent in bed and the kind of food that was eaten. Instead of a supervisor, the girls had an investigator, who kept records and organized the work. He explained everything he did, gave reasons, listened to comments and complaints, and did his best to secure a spirit of co-operation. The purpose of the experiment was carefully explained to the girls; absolutely nothing was concealed. They were asked to work comfortably and under no circumstances to rush. Throughout the experiment the purpose of the detailed changes was made clear; comment and criticism were invited; and noth-

ing was done without the consent of the girls, who even had the right of veto.

For the first month, in order to provide a basis for comparison, the girls worked under normal conditions. For the next twelve months or so, various experimental changes were made in working conditions, involving rest pauses, special meals, a shorter working day, and a five-day week. Production rose steadily as one improvement followed another. Then, with the consent of the girls, conditions reverted to normal for a period of three months: no rest pauses, no special meals, and a full-length working week. The astonishing thing was that, despite the removal of the improved conditions, both daily and weekly output rose during these three months to a higher level than before.

The first general conclusion, which became evident quite early in the investigation, was that although physical working conditions had an important effect on output, the relation was neither direct nor simple. It had at last dawned on a few industrialists that workers were not human machinery and that human beings plus machines gave not a mathematical, but a human equation.

The second conclusion was that the mental attitude of the girls was of paramount importance. The girls said that working in the Test-Room was fun; in particular, they liked being able to talk, which was not allowed in the department. It was a relief, they said, not to have a supervisor: they were able to breathe and get on with their work. There was no worry or anxiety. *They were not being watched.*

2. *The Interviewing Programme (1928–30).* The object was to obtain information about the attitudes of workers. Over 20,000 employees were interviewed, mostly by supervisors. The programme was a success: it gave the workers a chance to let off steam, with some therapeutic effect; and was excellent training for the supervisors, who became more understanding. The interviews, however, revealed many irrational and obsessive attitudes, and a general tendency of workers to gang together against anything they thought was a threat to their

well-being. Before any conclusions could be drawn from this, the Company needed to know how these attitudes affected the workers when they were on the job.

3. *The Bank Wiring Observation Room* (*1931–32*). The object was to study workers on the job under their own supervisor. There were to be no experimental changes; the method was observation pure and simple. Fourteen men engaged in the assembly of terminal banks for telephone exchanges were placed in a separate room with an observer. The men accepted the observer and spoke freely to him, but dried up completely when anyone in authority was about.

These men were paid according to an ingenious incentive scheme by which each could benefit from his own output and from that of the group as a whole, the assumption being that financial self-interest would keep everyone on the go and watchful of everyone else. Nothing of the sort happened; the observer found that the men had a fixed idea of a fair day's work: the wiring of two pieces of equipment and no more. As a consequence, the fastest workers slacked during the after-noon. Excess production was carried over to the next day, so that officially output never varied. The supervisor knew what was going on but was powerless to do anything about it. As a matter of fact there was little to complain of: the men were regarded by the firm as good honest workers and their produc-tion was well up to standard. Nevertheless, tests for skill and dexterity, which were made during the investigation, showed that the men were working below their capacity. There was an elaborate ritual against 'chisellers' and 'rate-busters', including the ceremony of 'binging', a symbolic blow on the arm of an offender to express the disapproval of the group.

Why was this? It appeared that the men had an unjustified fear that if they produced more their rate of pay would be cut.

INTERPRETATION: WHY WORKERS RESTRICT OUTPUT AND RESIST CHANGE

The girls in the Relay Assembly Test-Room increased out-put, even when the improved conditions were removed, because they enjoyed work which was a project requiring their *participation*, and because they were not supervised in the accepted sense. The investigator was permissive: what we would now call a democratic leader; not an authoritarian. Actually, the girls were under close supervision, but of a different kind, and subjected to constant change; but they were treated with the respect and trust that is taken for granted among members of a family.

Subsequent analysis of the records showed that the girls had developed a powerful community life. Their informal social organization was incredibly complex and totally unsuspected. For example, the output of friends often varied in the same way. Or again, when a girl nobody cared for was replaced by a girl everybody took to at once, output went down, not up, because the group had been disrupted; but rose to a higher level than before when the newcomer was integrated into the group. The men in the Bank Wiring Observation Room had an informal social organization as powerful and complex as that of the girls; but whereas the social relations of the girls made them co-operative and highly productive, that of the men made them resistant and restrictive. The difference was that change was *organized with* the girls but *imposed on* the men. The girls were treated like human beings: informed, consulted, and trusted. The men were not. Good pay, good conditions: what more could they want? They were treated like human machines.

What was happening in the Bank Wiring Observation Room was a pale reflection of what usually happens in industry. The working group acquires traditional skills and customary ways of doing things; the main satisfaction is the excellence of the work. Like any community, the working group has memories, loyalties, and expectations; and it needs the stimulus of challenge and participation. *But workers are constantly required to adapt their working customs and traditions to situations they do not understand, according to decisions in which they have had no part.* They feel that everything that makes them self-respecting members of a participative community is being threatened. To defend their integrity as human beings, they put up a strong resistance. This makes communication with management even more difficult, and leads to greater insecurity and greater resistance. The final result is a deep-seated hostility to management, opposition to change of any sort and restriction of output – usually quite unconscious.

THE IMPLICATIONS FOR MODERN INDUSTRY

The Hawthorne Investigations demolished the old conceptions: work was not necessarily unpleasant; workers were not isolated units; the carrot and the stick were not the only incentives; and workers were not governed solely by financial self-interest. This cleared the ground for an understanding of workers as *human beings*. Today, industrial behaviour is full of contradictions: genuine concern and crass indifference; neither one thing nor the other, an extraordinary ambivalence; and nowhere is this more apparent than in the attitude to change. All industrial countries are aware that technical change requires a new kind of supervision. This is a tremendous advance. But there is also a universal mood of uncomprehending toughness quite out of character with the science and sensitivity required for rapid development in a free world. Government control of industry is a case in point. There have been occasions in the histories of great democracies when many thousands of workers have been made redundant by the well-intentioned but autocratic decisions of their governments; and because the voters have had the final say, this has always been supposed to make the process democratic to the extent of justifying the total absence of prior consultation with those whose livelihood was at stake. The question is not whether these decisions were technically right or wrong: they were administratively inadequate, because the aspirations, fears, and contributions of the workers themselves were ignored. The contention that it would be inhuman to expect workers to participate in declaring their own redundancy is belied by some of the best consultative practice. The most revealing aspect of any discussion of the social cost of these vast redundancies is that there is never any mention of the cost of arbitrary methods, with their aftermath of resistance to change and restriction of output; nor is there the slightest allusion to the cost of inhibiting that inspired attitude to work which is only possible in communities where workers are respected.

The problem of free, participative societies is how to put large numbers of people to work so that no one is tyrannized by the processes of administration. The essential requirement is a moral conviction that systems are the ordering of social projects and must serve human ends. Our tentative industrial civilization has not yet learnt the lessons of the Hawthorne Investigations, particularly that change must be organized *with* those who are affected by it. It is a question of moral attitudes: whether those who work are to be respected as human beings or treated like things. The Hawthorne Investigations are a *moral* challenge.

---

finishing time

QUESTIONS

1 How did industrial psychologists and scientific managers think of workers?

2 What kind of employers were the Western Electric Company?

3 What happened at the Hawthorne Works when the workers thought the illumination had improved?

4 What was the purpose of the investigation in the Relay Assembly Test-Room?

5 Give *one* of the various experiment changes that were made in the working conditions of the girls in the Test-Room.

6 What happened to output when the improved conditions in the Test-Room were removed for a period of three months?

7 What was the first general conclusion of the investigators?

8 What was the attitude of these girls to working in the Test-Room?

9 Give *one* reason why the girls did not regard their investigator as a supervisor?

10 Give *one* piece of evidence to show that the girls had a complex social organization.

11 What led to the Interviewing Programme?

12 Mention *one* of the purposes of the Interviewing Programme?

13 What was the purpose of the investigation in the Bank Wiring Observation Room?

14 What conclusion was drawn from the tests for skill and dexterity?

15 What unjustified idea caused the men in the Observation Room to restrict output?

16 Give *one* of the old conceptions that were demolished by the Hawthorne Investigations.

17 According to the author, what is there about management's decision-making that causes hostility by the workers?

18 Mention *one* aspect of the social cost of making workers redundant on a vast scale by arbitrary methods.

19 What conclusion is reached about industrial change?

20 Why are the Hawthorne Investigations a moral challenge?

---

speed.........w.p.m. (page 243) comprehension.........(page 238)

Comments

Readers are inclined to forget the Interviewing Programme, because the account is short; it is, nevertheless, an integral part of the whole, and is emphasized in the synopsis (pages 202–3) of how the investigations developed. The example of government action is often overlooked, particularly by readers who do not agree with the interpretation.

Some groups have read a version of this article that was without headings, italics, and the synopsis of developments: their efficiency was very much reduced. There is a remarkably close connexion between the efficiency of reading and the way the material is presented.

Exercise 21 (1320 words)

THE NOISE ABOUT NOISE*

by Tom Margerison – *Sunday Times*, June 1963

starting time

The roar of traffic, the squeal of brakes, the clickety-clack of typewriters, the squeak of half-heard transistor radios, the pounding of machinery, the din of the jets. We live and work among it all. It disturbs sleep, frays tempers, reduces working efficiency, and does an unknown amount of actual physical harm. Noise has become the curse of modern civilisation.

But because it is the responsibility of nobody, because it is the by-product of almost every human activity, because being deaf is an affliction which fails to rouse human pity, the problem of controlling and limiting noise has been neglected. Only in the past few years, since the multiplication of the motor-car and the arrival of the strident-voiced jets, has the public conscience been aroused.

All over the world, communities are beginning to demand control of the onslaught on their ears. Rome and Paris banned the motor horn. Bermuda, whose peace was shattered a few years ago by the angry buzzing of mopeds, has clamped down on the noisiest of its proletarian transport. American motor manufacturers have agreed to limit the noise made by their cars. And the Port of New York Authority led the rest of the world in devising regulations to limit the quite unbearable noise of big jets taking off from Idlewild International Airport.

Now it is Britain's turn. A few days ago Mr Ernest Marples announced new draft regulations to control the ear-splitting roar of motor-cycles and sports cars, and to quieten the gruff voice of some heavy lorries. About the same time the Building Research Station revealed the disturbing results of its survey of noise in central London.

And on Tuesday, after three years' gestation, Sir Alan Wil-

* Reproduced by permission of the editor of the *Sunday Times*.

son's Committee on the Problem of Noise will report, in a White Paper, to the Minister for Science. It is not a snappy document. Its 250 pages read more like a university text book, with appendixes on scientific problems, and its dozen or so pages of recommendations call frequently for more research work.

Perhaps even more important is the survey being carried out over three years by the Medical Research Council and the Ministry of Pensions into the occupational hazards of noise.

For there is mounting evidence that at least one person in ten becomes deaf or partly deaf as a result of working in noisy surroundings. This is an aspect of noise which the Wilson Committee hardly touched upon. But it has immense social consequences.

Miss X, a woman of forty-five, worked in a cable factory on a noisy machine. She noticed she was going a little deaf and that the noise of the machine worried her less. Foolishly, she volunteered to work on a still more noisy machine. Then quite suddenly she discovered that she had become very deaf, that she was cut off from normal conversation.

In Britain (unlike many other countries) occupational deafness is not recognised as an industrial hazard, so that Miss X and others like her cannot obtain compensation for their disability. Deafness does not prevent a person from working, and may, in any case, have been due to disease or normal ageing rather than industrial noise.

Miss X was an exception. But thousands of people become partly deaf because of the noise made by the machines they work. The boiler-makers are the classic cases of industrial deafness, but lorry and bus drivers, steel workers, saw millers, and a host of others suffer too. Often the full effect only becomes obvious when the man retires. While he is working and his friends do the same job the whole group become used to shouting at one another. In the peace of retirement, the habit of shouting, of turning the wireless and television set too loud, becomes anti-social, and the deaf man finds it more difficult to fit into new surroundings.

The problem of industrial noise is that too few people care.

The hazard is not recognised, even by the people subjected to noise. The din is an unwanted and useless by-product, but one which is difficult and costly to remove. Take the case of the jet aircraft flying into London Airport. The noise they make is unpleasant enough for those who work at the airport, but even more so for those who live round about.

The nuisance could be reduced by moving the airport to some remote part of the country, but this would inconvenience air travellers and cost a great deal. The noise could be quietened by reducing the take-off weight of aircraft so that they rise more steeply and pass higher above the houses. But this would mean carrying fewer passengers, or less fuel, or both. The price of air tickets would have to rise, and airliners might have to make an intermediate stop on the route between London and New York, for example. More efficient 'mufflers' on the engines, or a new design of engine, might cut down noise a little. But usually there is a penalty. Mufflers add weight and reduce engine efficiency. Last year their use on B.O.A.C. airliners cost £400,000 in lost efficiency.

It is a matter of economic conflict between the public, largely disorganised but suffering a nuisance, and industry attempting to compete.

How much do people who live around noisy airports or near noisy factories really suffer? 'There are a few notorious streets near the airport,' said a Hounslow estate agent, 'where prices are £500 or £600 below what you'd expect.' But the Wilson Committee apparently failed to find these streets. In their view the desirable residences of Hounslow and other aircraft-ridden suburbs are snapped up as eagerly as elsewhere. Perhaps it is not unlike the Italian level-crossing keeper who slept through the earthquake that wrecked his house because he was so used to the trains going by.

Even so, 541 people complained about the noise around London Airport last year. And the Wilson Committee recommends that they should be given some help by the Government. Most of the noise comes in through the windows, so the proposal is to make grants to provide double windows and a sound-proof ventilation system costing round about £200 a room. Probably only a single room, the sitting-room, would be sound-proofed.

Public disturbance by noise from factories is usually less widespread, although the heavy thump of drop forges is even more disturbing than aircraft. The best solution in these cases is to site the noisy factories away from houses. Sir Alan Wilson calls for a schedule of these industrial noise producers.

For the rest, the noises fall into a different category. Next door's television set heard through the wall is a noise to me, although it may be a joy to my neighbour. The ding-dong of the ice-cream vendor is a delight to children, but infuriating to those who do not want or do not like ice-cream. One man's noise is another man's music.

Noises in this category are the inevitable result of close-living. They reflect, along with traffic noise, a fault in the design and construction of our towns. Standards of insulation between houses have to be improved. Properly enforced laws should forbid noisy advertising. City centres should be built to deaden the sound of traffic.

Now that the problem is beginning to be understood, the opportunities for quieter living are starting to become clear. But the present need is to train people who understand how to avoid and to deaden noise. Architects get little or no training in acoustics. Engineers have no idea how to design a machine which will be quiet. Even scientists with a knowledge of sound are in short supply.

The first step to a quieter world must be education. In Britain, there is not one university department of acoustics or noise control: a disgraceful record for one of the noisiest countries in the world.

---

finishing time

QUESTIONS

1 Give *two* reasons for the neglect of the problem of controlling and limiting noise.

2 There is mounting evidence that as a result of working in

213

noisy surroundings the proportion of people becoming deaf or partly deaf is (a) 1 in 10; (b) 1 in 20; (c) 1 in 50; (d) 1 in 100.

3 Compensation for occupational deafness (a) can be obtained in Britain, but not in other countries; (b) cannot be obtained in Britain, unlike many other countries; (c) cannot be obtained anywhere; (d) can be obtained in Britain, provided it can be proved – which is very difficult – that the disability arises from the work.

4 Give *one* of the possible ways of reducing the noise from aircraft and explain the drawback.

5 What does the Wilson Committee recommend to help those suffering from the noise around London Airport?

6 What is regarded as the best solution to the problem of public disturbance by noise from factories?

7 Mention *one* of the measures the author advocates for lessening the noises of close living.

8 Mention *two* main professions that need to provide special training for their members if the problem of noise is to be overcome.

9 What does the author say must be the first step to a quieter world?

---

speed.........w.p.m. (page 242) comprehension.........(page 239)

Exercise 22 (790 words)

Lord David Cecil, less despondent than Graham Hough,
sees literature as a means of attaining

WISDOM THROUGH DELIGHT*

---

starting time

Surely Mr Graham Hough is too despondent. No doubt teachers and students of English Literature at universities are a trifle

* Reproduced from the *Sunday Times*, March 1963, by permission of the editor.

dispirited these days, as are other people in England. Under-graduates do not read widely enough; and some dons – though not, I think, at Oxford – concentrate too much on producing professional critics and scholars and neglect the wants of their less gifted pupils.

Yet there is no reason to suggest, as Mr Hough does, that English Literature is a subject incurably at odds with the spirit of the age and should therefore be dropped.

From what I have seen round me at Oxford, and from my own personal experience as a teacher, I know that young people can still study literature enthusiastically and with profit. Why not? A book is the expression of a man; a good book is the expression of a remarkable man, and one, moreover, who can express himself with force and beauty. To read a university course in literature is to live for three years in the company of such men. This should be an enriching experience as well as an agreeable one.

And it has a special value today. People now tend to be prisoners of their period. They do not look outside it, they think its problems unique, they feel out of touch with any generation but their own. Studying literature destroys these illusions. We learn that the problems faced by past ages were just as difficult as ours and often much the same. We may find ourselves more in sympathy with some past author – Chaucer, perhaps, or Johnson – than with any contemporary.

Thus the study of literature enables the student to survey himself and his age in a longer perspective than before and with more detachment. Indeed, a literary education means an education in detachment. The reader must forget personal bias or prejudice if he is to enter into the minds of such a variety of people as are the authors of the past.

It is also a lesson in enjoyment; for all these authors have something to give him and he has failed in so far as he is un-receptive to any one of them. Here are some more precious lessons. Living, as we do, in a quarrelsome and anxious age, we need to redress the balance by cultivating detachment and the sense of pleasure.

If then young people do not respond to literature now, it

must be because it is wrongly presented to them. Some established modes of teaching are too formal and impersonal for today. The old full-dress lecture doesn't appeal as it used to. Young people prefer being taught singly or in small groups where they can intervene and ask questions; and where the teacher can vary his approach to suit the taste and temperament of his pupil. For it is no good forcing everyone down the same path. I deplore the tendency to concentrate on what are horribly called 'major' authors – Shakespeare, Milton, etc. – to the exclusion of others. Some people respond more easily to less exalted figures. The teacher should give them a chance to develop this response; nor should his tone be always solemn.

I suspect the teacher who talks about the duty of taking literature 'seriously'. Ardently, enthusiastically – Yes! But 'seriously' – No! Literature reflects life. It is questionable how much of life should be taken seriously.

Finally, the teacher must take care not to be too concerned with examination results. Such concern is a chief evil in university education today. It is a growing evil, too. Thirty years ago, austere and disinterested scholars spoke with scorn of any teacher who showed that he cared too intensely about how his pupils did in examinations. Now to do so is thought creditable.

There is a reason for this. People's jobs often depend on their degrees; the teacher who cares for his pupil's future cannot help worrying about his degree. All the same, it is a disastrous tendency. It disheartens the weak student and corrupts the strong; it leads both to work not at what they find most interesting and stimulating, but at what they think is most likely to get them high marks. The result is to kill their enthusiasm for their subject.

Every day we read how too much concern with the eleven plus examination strains children's nerves and withers their interest. So also does too much concern with examination results strain the nerves and wither the interest of undergraduates.

But, if it is taught sensibly and sympathetically and without undue reference to examinations, English Literature remains a subject which young people at universities will read with delight. And through delight they can – if they are capable of it – acquire wisdom.

finishing time

QUESTIONS

1 The author's opinion of undergraduates is that they (a) read indiscriminately; (b) do not read widely enough; (c) read only contemporary literature; (d) do not know their Shakespeare and Milton.   ( )

2 The attitude of some dons to less gifted pupils (though not, the author thinks, at Oxford) is (a) to neglect them; (b) to spend too much time on them; (c) to browbeat them; (d) to talk down to them.   ( )

3 The author criticizes Mr Graham Hough's suggestion that English Literature should be (a) a compulsory subject in all degree examinations; (b) an optional subject; (c) taught differently; (d) dropped.   ( )

4 Literature has a special value today because (a) the problems of the past were *human* problems, which do not change; (b) our outlook is universal; (c) we are prisoners of our period; (d) this is not a period of great literature.   ( )

5 Lord David Cecil's attitude to authors of the past is that (a) they can all give some pleasure to each one of us; (b) some speak to our condition, and some do not; (c) they had a longer perspective than authors today; (d) they were concerned with morality.   ( )

6 If young people do not respond to literature now, it must be because they are (a) too narrowly specialized; (b) not high-minded; (c) too detached; (d) wrongly taught.   ( )

7 Teachers should (a) teach their students to take life and literature more seriously; (b) acquaint students with less exalted literature; (c) not vary their approach to suit individual tastes and temperament; (d) concentrate more on major authors.   ( )

217

8   Scholars today should (a) aim at abolishing exami-
    nations; (b) care more about examination results; (c)
    not be too concerned with examination results; (d)
    aim at a different kind of examination.   (   )

9   The reason the author gives for his attitude to exam-
    inations is that (a) preoccupation with high marks
    kills the student's enthusiam for his subject; (b) stu-
    dents must be taught to take examinations in their
    stride, because life is a succession of tests; (c)
    examinations take no account of contemporary
    literature; (d) examinations strengthen the weak and
    encourage the strong.   (   )

10 Lord David Cecil concludes that if English Litera-
    ture is sensibly taught, young people will (a) become
    good and wise, even when they are not particularly
    gifted; (b) acquire wisdom through delight, whatever
    their capabilities; (c) respond with delight and learn
    not to take life seriously; (d) read with delight; and –
    if they are capable of it – acquire wisdom.   (   )

---

speed.........w.p.m. (page 241) comprehension.........(page 235)

PART IV

*

HOW MUCH IMPROVEMENT?

CHAPTER 13

THE FINAL EXERCISES

HERE, then, are the two final passages. The first, 'Slave Psychology Dying Hard', is comparable to 'The Fight Against the Dowry'; the second, 'Brave New World?', to 'Ends and Means'.

What to Do Next

Reading

In order to have the same conditions as for the initial exercises, do not preview.

Comprehension

Each passage has ten multiple-choice questions.

Exercise 23　　　　　(890 words)

SLAVE PSYCHOLOGY DYING HARD
SEX AND STATUS IN JAMAICA*
From the *Guardian*, December 1963

---

starting time

Jamaica, less than half a year after its achievement of full independence, is greatly agitated by two issues now being debated in its Parliament.

One is a proposal greatly to increase the penalties for rape; the other is a proposal to make compulsory the registration of the fathers of illegitimate children. These two issues have a common root in the racial situation. . . .

The African element, of course, is of slave descent, and the poorest and least educated of them still exhibit, to a large

* Reproduced by permission of the editor of the *Guardian*.

extent, what must be described as a slave psychology. It is shift-less, irresponsible, and sexually promiscuous.

There are, on the other hand, many others of African or partly African descent who copy the British pattern of culture in marital and other respects. The slave psychology disappears slowly, but it is declining, especially among the better educated.

During the days of slavery the education of slaves was legally prohibited. In spite of that, Christian missionaries from Britain worked among the slaves, and within a few years after the abolition of slavery in 1838 a stable middle class had emerged. They imitated their teachers and became known as 'pocket editions of Englishmen.'

In certain classes of society there is now a swing of the pendulum in the opposite direction, and there are strong attempts to cultivate an Africanism which is mostly bogus. There results a serious division in Jamaican society.

Social workers, who try to arrange adoptions for the numerous neglected children, often find that well-to-do people, whose own complexions may sometimes be very black, will accept children only with relatively fair skins and refuse the darker ones. . . .

The sexual looseness has deep roots in the past. Slave owners encouraged their female slaves to breed, or bred from them themselves, that being the cheapest and most convenient way of increasing the labour force on the sugar plantations. Paternity entailed no responsibilities, and slave women of high fecundity received special favours. As a result, at the present time, maternity among a large class is a matter to be proud of, regardless of marriage, whether legal or common law.

There are, however, others who are strictly monogamic though their unions are common law. The Rastafarians are said to be very faithful in this respect, though scorning legal marriage as a white man's institution. They do not realize that this whole situation is a legacy from slavery, under which slave marriages were illegal.

It is from this lowest social class that Jamaica's population explosion comes. Among them, church membership is a middle-class social symbol and they do not regard themselves as socially high enough to aspire to it. Marriage is not contemplated unless they feel that they have risen socially and have become members of the middle-class. Those who live in concubinage cannot become church members, and church membership is evidence of respectability.

The People's National Party, one of the two principal political parties, is affiliated to the Socialist International, but it has to prove its respectability, like its opponent, the Labour Party, by singing hymns and offering prayers at its meetings.

I was rather startled the first time I heard 'Nearer, my God, to Thee,' immediately followed by 'The People's Flag is Deepest Red.' The Labour Party recited the Apostles' Creed as well as singing hymns.

As soon as a couple become respectable enough to get legally married and join a church certain stresses develop. Most often it is the woman who is the first affected. As a married woman she feels she must have a maidservant. She must dress better and live in a better neighbourhood. If the husband's earnings remain the same, quarrels begin and the marriage is threatened.

A respected clergyman, who, however, felt reluctant to be quoted to that effect, told me he would be in favour of the legal recognition of common law marriages, or concubinage as he called it, at least to the extent of registering those couples who lived together as man and wife for a period exceeding 90 days. That would, he thought, give the churches an opportunity to accept such people and help them to cultivate a better way of life. At present they are antagonized and lack incentive to better themselves socially or religiously.

As things are, the poorest and least educated produce children recklessly. The slums in Jamaican towns are among the worst anywhere. Hovels are constructed out of old boxes, tin cans, and old discarded boards picked up from anywhere. In Kingston the worst area is known as Kingston Pen. Here the garbage from the town is thrown out, and both people and pigs search among it for scraps of food and anything else they can find. Some of these 'houses' have been torn down recently to make a road through the section.

Such are the problems this young nation has to grapple with.

HOW MUCH IMPROVEMENT?

The Government, through its Public Relations Office and its Tourist Bureau, presents to the world a picture of a glorious tropical island with wonderful scenery and everything to attract visitors. Hotels specially catering for tourists are springing up.... It may be added that the cost of living is lower than in Britain or the United States, and it is a wonderful place where one may retire, or go for a long holiday. But there is also another side to the picture.

---

finishing time

QUESTIONS

1 One of the recent proposals of the Jamaican Parliament was to make compulsory the registration of (a) illegitimate births; (b) unmarried couples; (c) adoptions; (d) fathers of illegitimate children. ( )

2 Slave psychology is described as (a) a conviction of inferiority; (b) irresponsibility and sexual promiscuity; (c) the acceptance of poverty; (d) a lack of independence and initiative. ( )

3 After the abolition of slavery in 1838 there emerged (a) a propertied upper class; (b) an educated upper class; (c) a stable middle class; (d) a lawless lower class. ( )

4 A serious division in Jamaican society has been caused by (a) religious extremists; (b) fanatical reformers; (c) a bogus Africanism; (d) political extremists. ( )

5 Sexual looseness has deep roots in the past because (a) religious fertility rites used to be practised; (b) slave owners were immoral; (c) slave owners would not allow their slaves to marry; (d) slave owners encouraged their female slaves to breed, or bred from them themselves. ( )

6 The Jamaican population explosion comes from (a) the middle class; (b) members of churches; (c) the

lowest social class; (d) those who live in concubinage. ( )

7 Marriage is (a) a lower-class institution; (b) a middle-class institution; (c) regarded as unnecessary by all classes; (d) binding only after the couple have lived together for ninety days. ( )

8 The sign of respectability is to (a) belong to a political party; (b) have many children; (c) belong to the church; (d) have a maidservant. ( )

9 A suggestion was made that people living in concubinage or accepting common-law marriage could be helped towards a better way of life if their situation was legally recognized. This was put forward by (a) the Labour Party; (b) the People's National Party; (c) social workers; (d) a clergyman. ( )

10 The cost of living is (a) lower than in Britain or the United States; (b) far higher than it should be, on account of the tourist trade; (c) rising so steeply that it is one of the main problems of this young nation; (d) an obstacle to marriage. ( )

speed.........w.p.m. (page 241) comprehension.........(page 236)

Exercise 24 (920 words)

BRAVE NEW WORLD?

Extract from *Brave New World Revisited** by Aldous Huxley

starting time

. . . We find ourselves confronted by a very disquieting question: Do we really wish to act upon our knowledge? Does a majority of the population think it worth while to take a good deal of trouble, in order to halt and, if possible, reverse the current drift towards totalitarian control of everything? In the United States – and America is the prophetic image of the rest of the urban-industrial world as it will be a few years from now – recent public opinion polls have revealed that an actual majority of young people in their teens, the voters of tomorrow, have no faith in democratic institutions, see no objection to the censorship of unpopular ideas, do not believe that government of the people by the people is possible, and would be perfectly content, if they can continue to live in the style to which the boom has accustomed them, to be ruled, from above, by an oligarchy of assorted experts. That so many of the well-fed young television-watchers in the world's most powerful democracy should be so completely indifferent to the idea of self-government, so blankly uninterested in freedom of thought and the right to dissent, is distressing, but not too surprising. 'Free as a bird', we say, and envy the winged creatures for their power of unrestricted movement in all the three dimensions. But, alas, we forgot the dodo. Any bird that has learned how to grub up a good living without being compelled to use its wings will soon renounce the privilege of flight and remain forever grounded. Something analogous is true of human beings. If the bread is supplied regularly and copiously three times a day, many of them will be perfectly content to live by bread alone – or at least by bread and circuses alone. 'In the end', says the Grand Inquisitor in Dostoevsky's parable, 'in the end they will lay their freedom at our feet and say to us, "Make us your slaves, but feed us."' And when Alyosha Karamazov asks his brother, the teller of the story, if the Grand Inquisitor is speaking ironically, Ivan answers: 'Not a bit of it! He claims it as a merit for himself and his Church that they have vanquished freedom and done so to make men happy.' Yes, to make men happy; 'for nothing', the Inquisitor insists, 'has ever been more insupportable for a man or a human society than freedom.' Nothing, except the absence of freedom; for when things go badly, and the rations are reduced and the slave drivers step up their demands, the grounded dodos will clamour again for their wings – only to renounce them, yet once more, when times grow better and the dodo-farmers become more lenient and generous. The young people who now think so poorly of democracy may grow up to become fighters for freedom. The cry 'Give me television and hamburgers, but don't bother me with the responsibilities of liberty', may give place, under altered circumstance, to the cry of 'Give me Liberty or give me death'. If such a revolution takes place, it will be due in part to the operation of forces over which even the most powerful rulers have very little control, in part to the incompetence of those rulers, their inability to make effective use of the mind-manipulating instruments with which science and technology have supplied, and will go on supplying, the would-be tyrant. Considering how little they knew and how poorly they were equipped, the Grand Inquisitors of earlier times did remarkably well. But their successors, the well-informed, thoroughly scientific dictators of the future, will undoubtedly be able to do a great deal better. The Grand Inquisitor reproaches Christ with having called upon men to be free and tells Him that 'we have corrected Thy work and founded it upon miracle, mystery and authority'. But miracle, mystery and authority are not enough to guarantee the indefinite survival of a dictatorship. In my fable of *Brave New World* the dictators had added science to the list and thus were able to enforce their authority by manipulating the bodies of embryos, the reflexes of infants, and the minds of children and adults. And instead of merely talking about miracles and hinting symbolically at mysteries, they were able, by means of drugs, to give their subjects the direct experience of mysteries and miracles – to transform mere faith into ecstatic knowledge. The older dictators fell because they could never supply their subjects with enough bread, enough circuses, enough miracles and mysteries. Nor did they possess a really effective system of mind-manipulation. In the past free-thinkers and revolutionaries were often the products of the most piously orthodox education. This is not surprising. The methods employed by orthodox educators were and still are extremely inefficient. Under a scientific dictator education will really work – with the result that most men and women will grow up to love their servitude and will never dream of revolution. There seems to be no good reason why a thoroughly scientific dictatorship should ever be overthrown.

HOW MUCH IMPROVEMENT?

Meanwhile there is still some freedom left in the world. Many young people, it is true, do not seem to value freedom. But some of us still believe that, without freedom, human beings cannot become fully human and that freedom is therefore supremely valuable. Perhaps the forces that now menace freedom are too strong to be resisted for very long. It is still our duty to do whatever we can to resist them.

finishing time

QUESTIONS

1 The current trend is towards (a) a profound questioning; (b) faith in science and technology; (c) totalitarian control; (d) unrestricted freedom. (   )

2 Recent public opinion polls in the United States showed that the majority of young people in their teens (a) had no faith in democratic institutions; (b) believed in democracy but were not interested in politics; (c) had nothing to offer but an attitude of dissent; (d) were beginning to lose faith in democracy. (   )

3 The United States is described as (a) a land governed by an oligarchy of assorted experts; (b) the world's most powerful democracy; (c) a land of grounded dodos; (d) a land ruled by big business. (   )

4 The aim of the Grand Inquisitor was (a) to make men happy by destroying their freedom; (b) to save from hell; (c) to protect the faithful; (d) to free mankind from worldly happiness. (   )

5 According to the *author*, nothing has ever been more insupportable than (a) boredom; (b) insecurity; (c) individual responsibility; (d) the absence of freedom. (   )

6 Young people who now think poorly of freedom may become (a) scientific dictators; (b) fighters for freedom; (c) organization men; (d) slaves to pleasure. (   )

7 Among other things, dictators of the future will undoubtedly be (a) philosophers; (b) financiers; (c) administrative geniuses; (d) mind manipulators. ( )

8 In the past the most piously orthodox education often produced revolutionaries because (a) its methods were extremely inefficient; (b) it was dogmatic; (c) it inspired to a life of service; (d) it inculcated discipline. ( )

9 A scientific dictatorship (a) is a contradiction in terms; (b) would be transformed by science itself; (c) may well be started by those who hate servitude; (d) could go on indefinitely. ( )

10 The forces that menace freedom (a) can only be counteracted by education for freedom; (b) may increase still further with the growth of materialism; (c) may be too strong to be resisted for very long; (d) should not be exaggerated, because most people value freedom. ( )

---

speed.........w.p.m. (page 241) comprehension.........(page 236)

CHAPTER 14

THE RESULTS

Making the Calculations

YOU calculate your percentage increase in speed (we can take an increase in speed for granted) and your percentage increase or decrease in comprehension. These calculations are quite simple. Follow the instructions, referring if necessary to the example, and enter the results in the spaces provided.

When you have done this we shall explain how to interpret the results.

A. *Average Initial Speed*
Add speeds Ex. 1 and Ex. 2; divide by 2   w.p.m.

B. *Average Final Speed*
Add speeds Ex. 23 and Ex. 24; divide by 2   w.p.m.

C. *Increase in Speed*
Subtract A from B   w.p.m.

D. **Percentage Increase in Speed**
Divide C by A; multiply by 100   per cent

E. *Average Initial Comprehension*
Add scores Ex. 1 and Ex. 2; divide by 2

F. *Average Final Comprehension*
Add scores Ex. 23 and Ex. 24; divide by 2

G. *Increase in Comprehension*
Subtract E from F

H. *Decrease in Comprehension*
Subtract F from E

I. **Percentage Increase in Comprehension**
Divide G by E; multiply by 100   per cent

J. **Percentage Decrease in Comprehension**
Divide H by E; multiply by 100   per cent

EXAMPLE

	Ex. 1	Ex. 2	Ex. 23	Ex. 24
SPEED	220	240	320	340
COMPREHENSION	70	80	80	80

A. *Average Initial Speed* $(220+240)\div2$ 230 w.p.m.

B. *Average Final Speed* $(320+340)\div2$ 330 w.p.m.

C. *Increase in Speed* $330-230$ 100 w.p.m.

D. **Percentage Increase in Speed** $\frac{100}{230}\times100$ 44 per cent

E. *Average Initial Comprehension* $(70+80)\div2$ 75

F. *Average Final Comprehension* $(80+80)\div2$ 80

G. *Increase in Comprehension*   5

I. **Percentage Increase in Comprehension** $\frac{5}{75}\times100$ 7 per cent

Suppose there had been a *decrease* in comprehension :

	Ex. 1	Ex. 2	Ex. 23	Ex. 24
	90	90	80	80

E. *Average Initial Comprehension*   90

F. *Average Final Comprehension*   80

H. *Decrease in Comprehension*   10

J. **Percentage Decrease in Comprehension** $\frac{10}{90}\times100$ 11 per cent

Interpreting the Results

1. Speed and comprehension should be considered together.

2. Nevertheless, for the great majority of readers the percentage increase in speed will be the significant index, because the aim of the training has been to read as fast as possible while maintaining a satisfactory level of comprehension.

3. Readers, however, will probably have increased their comprehension; and this will enhance their increase in speed. Or

the other hand, a decrease in comprehension will detract from their increase in speed.

4. If the reader starts with poor comprehension, an increase in comprehension may be the important factor.

5. This traditional method of testing is satisfactory as far as it goes; but you should bear in mind the limitations of this method, for as we stressed in the Introduction short tests cannot provide adequate scope for the strategy of reading.

A Final Word on Self-training

We have come to take improvement for granted and hope you are not disappointed with your results according to the tests.

You may wonder whether the improvement will be maintained. Follow-up tests give satisfactory results. But training is not something that is done once and for all: it is a continuing process. You have the approach and a knowledge of the methods; all your reading can now become a training activity that need not involve tiresome preoccupation, lack of spontaneity, and loss of enjoyment. But there is one condition: occasionally, very occasionally, you should turn whatever you are reading into a training exercise – make a conscious effort. If you do this, you should continue to improve.

APPENDICES

APPENDIX I

Key to Multiple-choice Questions

		Questions									
		1	2	3	4	5	6	7	8	9	10
1.	Ends and Means	d	b	a	c	b	b	d	c	a	c
2.	The Fight Against the Dowry	c	a	d	a	b	c	c	c	d	b
3.	Tears	b	b	a	b	d	b	c	b	a	a
4.	The Trouble with People	d	d	a	b	c	a	d	a	b	c
9.	Seeing and Believing	d	b	a	d	b	c	a	d	b	d
10.	Art and Artists	c	a	d	d	a	c	a	b	c	a
14.	Antidisestablishment-arianism	d	c	b	a	b	d	d	a	c	b
15.	Public Opinion	d	b	a	c	d	c	d	a	a	*
17.	Learning – An Irrational Process	b	c	d	c	a	a	d	c	a	c
18.	Tastes and Fashions of the Romantics	c	d	a	c	a	b	d	b	d	b
19.	The Road to Salvation	d	b	a	d	a	b	a	c	a	d
22.	Wisdom Through Delight	b	a	d	c	a	d	b	c	a	d

* Freedom of information; freedom of dissent; freedom from victimization; freedom to exert influence.

Key to Multiple-choice Questions (continued)

		Questions									
		1	2	3	4	5	6	7	8	9	10
23.	Slave Psychology Dying Hard	d	b	c	c	d	c	b	c	d	a
24.	Brave New World?	c	a	b	a	d	b	d	a	d	c

APPENDIX II

Key to Free-answer Questions

THE following answers are a *guide* and should not be taken literally; consult the text to see if you have grasped the general meaning. *The marks for each question are given in brackets.*

EXERCISE 5

1. We are simultaneously aware of the parts and of their relationships ($1\frac{1}{2}$). 2. Express complex ideas in a linear sequence ($1\frac{1}{2}$). 3. Reconstruct (understand) the whole meaning from the sequence (line) ($1\frac{1}{2}$). 4. How knowledge is communicated. Similar to transmission – picture broken up; and to reception – appearance of unity ($1\frac{1}{2}$). 5. It is what we do spontaneously with any material we find interesting ($1\frac{1}{2}$). 6. If he is afraid of forgetting, he is likely to forget ($1\frac{1}{2}$). 7. To understand (1).

EXERCISE 6

1. They have lacked amenities (1). 2. Everyone prefers to have a home of his own (1); high cost per unit of accommodation (1). 3. Higher cost of services (1); time and money for travelling (1). 4. (a) Young people (students) ($\frac{1}{2}$); young married people ($\frac{1}{2}$); those who must live near their work ($\frac{1}{2}$); retired people ($\frac{1}{2}$). 4. (b) Married couples with children living at home (1). We must plan to get the right proportion of the different types of home (2).

EXERCISE 7

1. Regular practice (1). 2. Insufficient training (1). 3. Anticipation (1). 4. Vigilance (1). 5. (b) (1). 6. (a) (1). 7. (a) (1). 8. (d) (1). 9. He may be anti-social – aggressive or intolerant of authority (1). 10. They become safer drivers (1).

EXERCISE 8

1. The dam at Aswan (1). 2. The doubling of the population (1). 3. Negligible (1). 4. Industrialization (1). 5. *Two* of the following ($\frac{1}{2}$ mark each): revenues of the Suez Canal; nationalization (and expropriation) of foreign firms; Russian aid. 6. (b) (1). 7. Oil (1). 8. (b) (1). 9. The increase in population (1). 10. (b) (1).

EXERCISE 16

1. Complete devotion to country (1). 2. Displayed before judges; if unfit, condemned to exposure (1). 3. (a) Boarding school – juvenile barracks ($\frac{1}{2}$). 3. (b) Military training ($\frac{1}{2}$). 4. Obedience (1). 5. (a) To encourage stealing ($\frac{1}{2}$). 5. (b) Being caught stealing ($\frac{1}{2}$). 6. Political assassination (1). 7. Physical (and pre-military) fitness (1). 8. Very little – just enough to serve their turn (1). 9. To encourage a martial spirit (1). 10. To learn to express themselves laconically – briefly (1).

EXERCISE 20

($\frac{1}{2}$ mark for each question)

1. As human machines. 2. Good. 3. Output increased. 4. To study the connexion between physical working conditions and production *or* the effect on output of changes in working conditions. 5. *One* of the following: rest pauses; special meals; a shorter working day; a five-day week. 6. It rose. 7. The relation between output and working conditions was not a direct one; not a simple one. 8. It was fun; relief not to have a supervisor; felt no worry; felt they were not being watched; etc. 9. They were treated like human beings; they were respected; the investigator was permissive; he encouraged them to participate; etc. 10. *One* of the following: the output of friends varied in the same way; newcomer nobody liked – output fell, but rose later. 11. The Company knew little about workers as human beings. 12. To study workers as human beings *or* to obtain information about the attitudes of the workers. 13. To observe workers on the job under their supervisor. 14. The men were working below capacity. 15. The fear that their rate of pay

would be cut if they produced more. 16. *One* of the following: work was unpleasant; workers were isolated units; the only incentive was the carrot or the stick; financial self-interest was the only motive. 17. It does not involve the workers in decisions that affect their traditions. 18. *One* of the following: resistance to change; restriction of output; no inspired attitude to work. 19. It must be organized *with* those who are affected by it; and should not be imposed on them. 20. Because they show that workers must be respected as human beings.

EXERCISE 21

1. *Two* of the following (1 mark each): responsibility of nobody; by-product of almost every human activity; deafness fails to rouse pity. 2. (a) (1). 3. (b) (1). 4. *One* of the following ($\frac{1}{2}$ mark for the possible way; $\frac{1}{2}$ mark for the explanation): remove airport – cost and inconvenience; reduce weight of aircraft – fewer passengers, less fuel; mufflers – increased weight *or* loss of efficiency. 5. Grants for the sound-proofing of homes (1). 6. Build factories away from houses (1). 7. *One* of the following (1): better insulation between houses; laws against noisy advertising; towns designed to deaden the sound of traffic. 8. Architecture; engineering ($\frac{1}{2}$ mark each). 9. Education (1).

APPENDIX III

Table of Speeds

Time in Seconds	Speed in w.p.m.					
	Ex. 1	Ex. 2	Ex. 3	Ex. 4	Ex. 5	Ex. 6
60	910	900	970	1150	880	940
70	780	771	831	986	754	806
80	683	675	728	863	660	705
90	607	600	647	767	587	627
100	546	540	582	690	528	564
110	496	490	529	629	480	513
120	455	450	485	575	440	470
130	420	415	448	531	406	434
140	390	386	416	493	377	403
150	364	360	388	460	352	376
160	341	338	364	431	330	353
170	321	318	342	406	311	332
180	303	300	323	383	293	313
190	287	284	306	363	278	297
200	273	270	291	345	264	282
210	260	257	277	329	251	269
220	248	245	265	314	240	256
230	237	235	253	300	230	245
240	228	225	243	288	220	235
250	218	216	233	276	211	226
260	210	208	224	265	203	217
270	202	200	216	256	196	209
280	195	193	208	246	189	201
290	188	186	201	238	182	194
300	182	180	194	230	176	188
310	176	174	188	223	170	182
320	171	169	182	216	165	176
330	165	164	176	209	160	171

TABLE OF SPEEDS

Time in Seconds	Speed in w.p.m.					
	Ex. 1	Ex. 2	Ex. 3	Ex. 4	Ex. 5	Ex. 6
340	161	159	171	203	155	166
350	156	154	166	197	151	161
360	152	150	162	192	147	157
370	148	146	157	186	143	152
380	144	142	153	182	139	148

Time in Seconds	Speed in w.p.m.						
	Ex. 7	Ex. 15	Ex. 17	Ex. 19	Ex. 22	Ex. 23	Ex. 24
60	1200	1060	920	980	790	890	920
70	1029	909	789	840	677	763	789
80	900	795	690	735	593	668	690
90	800	707	613	653	527	593	613
100	720	636	552	588	474	534	552
110	655	578	502	535	431	485	496
120	600	530	460	490	395	445	460
130	554	489	425	452	365	411	425
140	514	454	394	420	339	381	394
150	480	424	368	392	316	356	368
160	450	398	345	368	296	334	345
170	424	374	325	346	279	314	325
180	400	353	307	327	263	297	307
190	379	335	291	309	249	281	291
200	360	318	276	294	237	267	276
210	343	303	263	280	226	254	263
220	327	289	251	267	215	243	251
230	313	277	240	256	206	232	240
240	300	265	230	245	198	223	230
250	288	254	221	235	190	214	221
260	277	245	212	226	182	205	212
270	267	236	204	218	176	198	204
280	257	227	197	210	169	191	197
290	248	219	190	203	163	184	190
300	240	212	184	196	158	178	184

Time in Seconds	Speed in w.p.m.						
	Ex. 7	Ex. 15	Ex. 17	Ex. 19	Ex. 22	Ex. 23	Ex. 24
310	232	205	178	190	153	172	178
320	225	199	173	184	148	167	173
330	218	193	167	178	144	162	167
340	212	187	162	173	139	157	162
350	206	182	158	168	135	153	158
360	200	177	153	163	132	148	153
370	195	172	149	159	128	144	149
380	189	167	145	155	125	141	145

Time in Seconds	Speed in w.p.m.						
	Ex. 8	Ex. 10	Ex. 13	Ex. 14	Ex. 16	Ex. 18	Ex. 21
120	690	720	660	760	685	685	660
130	637	664	609	702	632	632	609
140	591	617	566	651	587	587	566
150	552	576	528	608	548	548	528
160	518	540	495	570	514	514	495
170	487	508	466	536	484	484	466
180	460	480	440	507	457	457	440
190	436	455	417	480	433	433	417
200	414	432	396	456	411	411	396
210	394	411	377	434	391	391	377
220	376	393	360	415	374	374	360
230	360	376	344	397	357	357	344
240	345	360	330	380	343	343	330
250	331	346	317	365	329	329	317
260	318	332	305	351	316	316	305
270	307	320	293	338	304	304	293
280	296	309	283	326	294	294	283
290	286	298	273	314	283	283	273
300	276	288	264	304	274	274	264
310	267	279	255	294	265	265	255
320	259	270	248	285	257	257	248

TABLE OF SPEEDS

Time in Seconds	Speed in w.p.m.						
	Ex. 8	Ex. 10	Ex. 13	Ex. 14	Ex. 16	Ex. 18	Ex. 21
330	251	262	240	276	249	249	240
340	244	254	233	268	242	242	233
350	237	247	226	261	235	235	226
360	230	240	220	253	228	228	220
370	224	234	214	246	222	222	214
380	218	227	208	240	216	216	208
390	212	222	203	234	211	211	203
400	207	216	198	228	206	206	198
410	202	211	193	222	200	200	193
420	197	206	189	217	196	196	189

Time in Seconds	Speed in w.p.m.				Time in Seconds	Speed in w.p.m.	
	Ex. 9	Ex. 11	Ex. 12	Ex. 20		Ex. 12	Ex. 20
120	880	975	1695	1280	550	370	279
130	812	900	1565	1182	560	363	274
140	754	836	1453	1097	570	357	269
150	704	780	1356	1024	580	351	265
160	660	731	1271	960	590	345	260
170	621	688	1196	904	600	339	256
180	587	650	1130	853	610	333	252
190	556	616	1071	808	620	328	248
200	528	585	1017	768	630	323	244
210	503	557	969	731	640	318	240
220	480	532	925	698	650	313	236
230	459	509	884	668	660	308	233
240	440	488	848	640	670	304	229
250	422	468	814	614	680	299	226
260	406	450	782	591	690	295	223
270	391	433	753	569	700	291	219
280	377	418	726	549	710	286	216
290	364	403	701	530	720	283	213
300	352	390	678	512	730	279	210

Time in Seconds	Speed in w.p.m.				Time in Seconds	Speed in w.p.m.	
	Ex. 9	Ex. 11	Ex. 12	Ex. 20		Ex. 12	Ex. 20
310	341	377	656	495	740	275	208
320	330	366	636	480	750	271	205
330	320	355	616	465	760	268	202
340	311	344	598	452	770	264	199
350	302	334	581	439	780	261	197
360	293	325	565	427	790	257	194
370	285	316	550	415	800	254	192
380	278	308	535	404	810	251	190
390	271	300	522	394	820	248	187
400	264	293	509	384	830	245	185
410	258	285	496	375	840	242	183
420	251	279	484	366	850	239	181
430	246	272	473	357	860	237	179
440	240	266	462	349	870	234	177
450	235	259	452	341	880	231	175
460	230	254	442	334	890	229	173
470	225	249	433	327	900	226	171
480	220	244	424	320	910	223	169
490	215	239	415	313	920	221	167
500	210	234	407	307	930	219	165
510	207	229	399	301	940	216	163
520	203	225	391	295	950	214	162
530	199	221	384	290	960	212	160
540	195	217	377	284	970	209	159

APPENDIX IV

Record Sheet

Comprehension (Maximum 100: multiply score by 10)	Speed in w.p.m.	Exercise	
90	200	1	Ends and Means
80	190	2	The Fight Against the Dowry
		3	Tears
		4	The Trouble with People
		5	Look at a Threepenny-Piece
		6	Flats Versus Houses
		7	The Driver and Other Road Users
		8	Resources of the Nile
		9	Seeing and Believing
		10	Art and Artists
		11	Universal Histories
		12	Bell Telephone's Experiment
		13	Contract for a Wireless Set
		14	Antidisestablishmentarianism
		15	Public Opinion

Comprehension (*Maximum 100: Multiply score by 10*)	Speed in w.p.m.	Exercise	
		16	Spartan Training
		17	Learning – An Irrational Process
		18	Tastes and Fashions of the Romantics
		19	The Road to Salvation
		20	The Hawthorne Investigations
		21	The Noise about Noise
		22	Wisdom Through Delight
		23	Slave Psychology Dying Hard
		24	Brave New World?

APPENDIX V

Mechanical Aids to Training – An Assessment

Mechanical aids fall into two categories: devices for widening the visual span; and pacing devices.

1. *Devices for Widening the Visual Span*

Those who employ such aids assume, quite wrongly in our opinion, that if the reader is trained to see isolated spans – to get a 'good eyeful' – he will read better. These devices are of two kinds:

The tachistoscope – an instrument which flashes a span of words on to a screen for a fraction of a second.

The flasher – usually no more than a piece of cardboard in which an oblong window has been cut; the reader flashes the card over the text, exposing a span of words through the window. There are also more elegant devices which work on the same principle.

Neither the tachistoscope nor the flasher is of value because, as we have already explained in Chapter 5, p. 82, the reader has phenomenal visual capacity: the slow reader, in fact, sees the print many times over because his spans overlap so much (Fig. 3, p. 80).

It may be argued that the tachistoscope and the flasher widen the span of *attention*; but if attention is too narrow, the difficulty is not one of 'seeing', but of *reading*; and no amount of practice with isolated spans can help the reader to relate a succession of spans and organize their meaning.

2. *Pacing Devices*

Pacing can be a valuable stimulus. (The timing of reading exercises is, of course, a form of pacing.) The danger of the two kinds of a mechanical pacer – the reading machine and the reading film – is that the psychological advantages of an external stimulus, which gives speed, may be outweighed by the inevitable disadvantages of a mechanical method, which, by inducing a habit of inflexibility, may impair comprehension.

READING MACHINES

The most popular kind of machine is a contrivance with an opaque sheet or bar that passes down the page covering the text line by line; the machine can be set to any speed. Another kind is a cabinet with a built-in screen, in appearance rather like a small television set; a film is placed in the cabinet and the text projected on to the screen line by line; this machine can also be set to any speed.

Reading machines, like all pacing devices, oblige the reader to proceed rhythmically, at an even speed, and without regressing. In our opinion, these are serious disadvantages because the reader is unable to read flexibly and cannot, therefore, distribute his effort economically. As for regression, the evidence is that it cannot be prevented by concealing the words (Chapter 5, p. 82).

READING FILMS

The Harvard University reading films are a highly sophisticated pacing device. There are sixteen films which are projected on to a large screen, so that a group of readers can participate in the training. The films cover a range of speed from slow to fast; though the speed of the individual film is constant. The text is made visible in a succession of spans or 'fixations'. The slow films have five fixations per line; the fast films, two fixations per line.

We ourselves use the Harvard films because we value them as a pacing device and because they introduce an element of variety. We are very careful, however, to explain their shortcomings; and we encourage readers to be critical of the method. Readers, for example, find that the individual film appears to vary in speed: they come to realize that when the meaning is difficult the film seems to speed up, and when the meaning is easy it seems to slow down – a powerful demonstration of the principle of flexibility. Again, when they have read a particular two-fixation film, they assume that their eyes have made two fixations per line; but when it is pointed out to them that in this film the duration of each fixation is $\frac{1}{2}$ second and that they have certainly made four fixations per line (at the normal $\frac{1}{4}$ second), they realize that they are unable to tell what their eyes are doing.

With this kind of approach, readers are able to benefit from the stimulus of pacing and yet safeguard themselves against the acquisition of bad reading habits.

Conclusions

1. Devices for widening the visual span serve no purpose; the evidence is that they neither increase speed nor improve comprehension.

2. Mechanical pacing devices are expendable; we ourselves have obtained equally good results without using the Harvard films. Pacing devices are a danger in that they can easily increase speed at the expense of comprehension. If they are used, they should not be the sole method; they should always be a subordinate part of training; and the reader should be made aware of their limitations and trained to recognize their deficiencies. It follows from this that pacing devices need expert handling.

THE PSYCHOLOGY OF LEARNING

Robert Borger and A. E. M. Seaborne

Only a small part of learning takes place in schools. Just as a child learns to walk, talk, and handle things without the help of trained teachers, so industrial skills are normally acquired by imitation and practice. Learning, in fact, takes place all the time, without anyone setting out either to learn or teach.

Two psychologists discuss in this Pelican the laws which seem to govern the process of learning in its widest sense. The theories and models which have been based on simple learning situations are their first consideration; but they also provide a thorough survey of programmed learning techniques and the newer developments in the formal teaching of schools and universities.

Those in the front line of education are perhaps only just beginning to pay systematic attention to psychological studies of learning. With the view it opens up of the whole field of human and animal learning, this book can be of fundamental assistance to them.

THE PSYCHOLOGY OF PERCEPTION

M. D. Vernon

When we look at the world with our eyes, do we see it *as it really is?* In this authoritative study the Professor of Psychology at the University of Reading shows how, behind the retina of the eye, many more fallible mental processes cause errors and inconsistencies to creep into our perceptions. We are seldom aware of these.

Here then is a non-technical outline of the psychological processes which have been shown to be involved in our visual perceptions of things around us. These perceptions of shape, colour, movement, and space develop gradually from infancy upwards. Special processes also emerge to enable us to deal with symbolic material such as printed words and diagrams, for the purpose, in particular, of reading. Finally this book, which is based on over thirty years of psychological research at Cambridge and elsewhere, shows how the perceptions of different people are not always alike: they vary with attention, interest, and individual personality factors.

WRITING TECHNICAL REPORTS

Bruce M. Cooper

'A lively and thoroughly practical attempt to show how technical information may be written and presented so that it is easy to read and understand' – *The Times Educational Supplement*

This Pelican offers to scientists, engineers, and others the main principles of writing a technical report, from first draft to final version.

Bruce Cooper, who is currently engaged in management training for a large chemical firm, maintains that a report needs to be more than a vehicle for recording exact information. It is, in fact, an exercise in human relations, in which clarity is certainly as important as correctness. The varying outlooks of the potential readers must be considered as thoroughly as the factual contents of the report.

Arguing strongly for personal involvement by the writer – to the extent, if necessary, of employing the first person singular – the author gives advice on the structure of the whole report, on grammar, on the construction of sentences, on the choice of vocabulary and the avoidance of mere jargon, and on punctuation. His chapters are effectively illustrated with quotations from published technical papers and reports.

PENGUIN REFERENCE BOOKS

The Penguin English Dictionary

Over 1,000 pages long and with over 68,000 definitions, this cheap, compact and totally up-to-date book is ideal for today's needs. It includes many technical and colloquial terms, guides to pronunciation and common abbreviations.

The Penguin Reference Dictionary

The ideal comprehensive guide to written and spoken English the world over, with detailed etymologies and a wide selection of colloquial and idiomatic usage. There are over 100,000 entries and thousands of examples of how words are actually used – all clear, precise and up-to-date.

The Penguin English Thesaurus

This unique volume will increase anyone's command of the English language and build up your word power. Fully cross-referenced, it includes synonyms of every kind (formal or colloquial, idiomatic and figurative) for almost 900 headings. It is a must for writers and utterly fascinating for any English speaker.

The Penguin Dictionary of Quotations

A treasure-trove of over 12,000 new gems and old favourites, from Aesop and Matthew Arnold to Xenophon and Zola.

FOR THE BEST IN PAPERBACKS, LOOK FOR THE 🐧

PENGUIN REFERENCE BOOKS

The Penguin Guide to the Law

This acclaimed reference book is designed for everyday use, and forms the most comprehensive handbook ever published on the law as it affects the individual.

The Penguin Medical Encyclopedia

Covers the body and mind in sickness and in health, including drugs, surgery, history, institutions, medical vocabulary and many other aspects. 'Highly commendable' – *Journal of the Institute of Health Education*

The Penguin French Dictionary

This invaluable French-English, English-French dictionary includes both the literary and dated vocabulary needed by students, and the up-to-date slang and specialized vocabulary (scientific, legal, sporting, etc) needed in everyday life. As a passport to the French language, it is second to none.

A Dictionary of Literary Terms

Defines over 2,000 literary terms (including lesser known, foreign language and technical terms) explained with illustrations from literature past and present.

The Penguin Map of Europe

Covers all land eastwards to the Urals, southwards to North Africa and up to Syria, Iraq and Iran. Scale – 1:5,500,000, 4-colour artwork. Features main roads, railways, oil and gas pipelines, plus extra information including national flags, currencies and populations.

The Penguin Dictionary of Troublesome Words

A witty, straightforward guide to the pitfalls and hotly disputed issues in standard written English, illustrated with examples and including a glossary of grammatical terms and an appendix on punctuation.